"I applaud its overall thrust as very true and timely."
> Dr. J. I. Packer—Professor of Systematic and Historical Theology, Regent College, Vancouver, B.C.

"The book is full of grand insights."
> Rev. Armin Gesswein—Founder and Director of Revival Prayer Fellowship, Inc., California.

"I hope that this message is heard and heeded by the Church."
> Dr. Robert E. Coleman—Professor of Evangelism, Asbury Theological Seminary.

"A word from the Lord for all His Body."
> Norman Grubb—Author and Missionary.

"The book is great. Just what we need at this time in the Christian Community."
> Arthur Blessitt—Of Cross-carrying fame.

"Heart piercing and thought provoking."
> Chuck Smith—Pastor of Calvary Chapel, Costa Mesa, California.

LOVE
COVERS

LOVE COVERS

A BIBLICAL DESIGN FOR UNITY IN THE BODY OF CHRIST

PAUL E. BILLHEIMER

BETHANY HOUSE PUBLISHERS
MINNEAPOLIS, MINNESOTA 55438
A Division of Bethany Fellowship, Inc.

CHRISTIAN LITERATURE CRUSADE
Fort Washington, Pennsylvania 19034

Co-published by
Bethany House Publishers and
Christian Literature Crusade

Printed in the United States of America

Library of Congress Cataloging in Publication Data

Billheimer, Paul E.
  Love covers.

  Includes bibliographical references.
  1. Christian union. 2. Love (Theology)   I. Title.
BX8.2.B46   1983   262'.0011   83-15823
ISBN 0-87123-400-9 (pbk.)

ENDORSEMENT

Here is a word that will sting, rebuke, and disturb, but *in the end, I predict, will bless.* It is likely that you will not agree with everything in this volume. It is just as likely that you need not agree with everything herein to be benefitted by it.

In his usual style, Paul E. Billheimer captures the true essence of the issue in the religious world today and lays bare the bones of contention with rare grace. His practice of overall fairness to all may be unnerving to some. To many of his observations you will say an immediate "Amen!" To others, you will say a painful "O me!"

Read it through without argument. Then feel free to put its contents to the scriptural test. That will be much less painful than running it through the denominational filter.

You will hurt, you will doubtless feel some irritation, and you may even weep a little. You may rise to argue a point, you may sink to some despair, but eventually you will be blessed if you wait for the Spirit's "Amen!"

I commend this book to your studied attention.

Dr. Jack R. Taylor
President of
Dimensions in Christian Living

Author and Evangelist

DEDICATION

To all my descendants who, it appears, are members of the *terminal or rapture generation.*

With loving appreciation to my wife of sixty-one years, without whose loyal, faithful, and efficient assistance our publishing and television ministries would be impossible.

MY THANKS TO:

Norma Aspin for reproducing the manuscript.

Dick Eastman for valuable editorial suggestions and assistance.

David Shibley for literary editing and typing in preparation for publication.

PREFACE

The most important, momentous, crucial, but the most ignored, neglected, and unsolved problem that has faced the Church from its infancy to the present throbbing moment is the problem of disunity. The continuous and widespread fragmentation of the Church has been the scandal of the ages. It has been Satan's master strategy. The sin of disunity probably has caused more souls to be lost than all other sins combined. Possibly more than anything else, it is the one thing that binds the hands of the Holy Spirit and thwarts His work of convincing of sin, righteousness and judgment.

On the Day of Pentecost the Holy Spirit came when the Church was in full accord. Since then He has operated only in the ambience of love and fellowship. Therefore, without doubt, the most important prerequisite to world evangelization and revival is the unity of the Body of Christ.

What is the basis for the fellowship which represents, defines, and gives content to this unity? According to *Webster's New World Dictionary,* the term "fellow" from the word "fellowship" denotes ultimate identical derivation. In other words, two persons being designated as fellows implies common origin, a common family relationship. Therefore the primary, fundamental and distinguishing basis for fellowship is shared ancestry rather than shared theories, concepts or opinions.

7

If this means anything at all it means that fellowship between born-again believers, members of the same family, should be on the basis of a common spiritual parentage rather than common opinions on nonessentials to salvation.

For centuries, fellowship within the Body of Christ has been primarily on the basis of conceptual, theological and organizational persuasions and practices. The principal thesis of this book is that in the Church, or Body of Christ, acceptance and fellowship with one another should be on the basis of common spiritual parentage rather than on common views or opinions in nonessentials to salvation.

What constitutes beliefs necessary to salvation may be controversial. It is unclear to *me,* for instance, how anyone can be born again without acceptance of the Word of God in its original autographs as inerrant. This may seem an arbitrary definition of an essential belief for salvation. Yet, to me, it is of great importance.

At a conference called a "summit" of the International Council on Biblical Inerrancy, held in Chicago on October 26-28, 1978, and reported in the November 17 issue of *Christianity Today,* the Council declared that biblical authority cannot be maintained if biblical inerrancy is denied. Although the Chicago statement of inerrancy affirmed that the authority of Scripture is "inescapably impaired if total divine inerrancy is in any way limited or disregarded," the statement does *not* insist that belief in inerrancy is necessary for salvation. So for that reason I shall not. But rejectors *are* warned of "serious loss to both the individual and the Church."

For the purpose of this book, the term "essentials to salvation" will be considered as the minimum beliefs necessary for the new birth. According to the Apostle John, no one can have saving faith who does not believe in the unique Sonship of Jesus. "If anyone acknowledges that Jesus is the Son of God, God lives in him and he in God....Everyone who believes that Jesus is the Christ is born of God, and everyone who loves the father loves his child as well" (1 John 4:15; 5:1 *NIV*).

Perhaps the simplest confession of evangelical faith or faith for conversion is found in Romans 10:9-10: "That if you shall confess with your mouth 'Jesus is Lord,' and believe in your heart that God raised him from the dead, you will be saved. For it is with your heart you believe and are justified, and it is with your mouth that you confess and are saved" (*NIV*).

In this book, the term "nonessentials to salvation" will then be understood as doctrinal matters not related distinctly or directly to the new birth.

It is only natural that the measure or dimension of fellowship may be affected by the degree of agreement or disagreement on various phrases of divergent theological positions. But fellowship based on a common family relationship through the new birth should properly overshadow or even dwarf fellowship based on opinions not essential to divine life. In other words, membership in the same family is a more important foundation for fellowship, especially to the heavenly Father, than intellectual or theological agreement. This is because all members of God's family are equally precious to Him. So far as He is concerned, no difference in opinions on nonessentials to the new birth justifies alienation in the family If assumed error does not produce broken fellowship between the heavenly Father and one of His born-again children, is there any reason it should do so between brothers and sisters?

This does not require the abandonment or the compromise of vital principles. It is not a plea to relinquish or reduce any convictions. No one has to give up any precept, persuasion, or canon of faith to love a "blood-bought brother." It is an appeal to cease making one's opinions on nonessentials the basis for fellowship or unity in the Spirit.

Neither does this mean that truth in these beliefs is unimportant. It does mean that, in God's sight, relationship is *supremely* important. It does not mean that such error may not damage the Body. It does mean that breaking fellowship over beliefs not vital to the new birth does more damage to the Body than the error that caused the break.

Again, this does not mean that the search for truth in other areas of doctrine is wrong. Neither does it mean that having one's own opinion is wrong. It does not even mean that earnestly contending for one's opinion in these matters of doctrine is a sin. This is not where the problem lies. In God's sight, the wrong is in allowing opinions to cause a breach of fellowship between born-again members of the same family. This is a violation and repudiation of the heart cry of Jesus in John chapter 17, and that is sin.

According to Church history, the Church has never clearly seen at any one period the supreme importance of this truth. Can this be the one thing that has delayed the fulfillment of the Great Commission and prevents Christ's glorious return? If so, should not every lover of Jesus give highest priority to His prayer in John 17, "...that they may be one as we are one"?

CONTENTS

Satan's Trap

FOREWORD

For nearly two thousand years the prayer of Jesus in John 17:21 has awaited fulfillment: "Father, that they may be one...." For years, congregations have stood and with great fervor sung the familiar line from the grand marching-hymn of Christendom, "Onward, Christian Soldiers": "We are not divided, all one body we." And yet the real fulfillment of this great hymn has been only an illusive, heart-rending dream. As Paul Billheimer exhorts us in this historic writing, LOVE COVERS, the greatest sin of the Church of Jesus Christ is disunity.

But, praise God, a new breath of the Holy Spirit is blowing across the land! Hard evidence that Jesus' prayer is being answered is coming in. "Washington for Jesus" of 1980 saw half a million members of Christ's Body joined together by one common denominator—*love*—love for Jesus Christ and love for one another. Many other great convocations were held that year, and many more are in the planning as we move into the decade of the 80's. I have seen Baptists hugging Pentecostals—Presbyterians and Catholics praying together in the Spirit—Lutherans and Nazarenes laughing and praising God, as each laid aside doctrinal and denominational differences in love.

Jesus said, "By this shall all men know that you are my disciples, if you have love for one another."

Paul Billheimer's book herewith presented will, no doubt, be one of the great keys which the Holy Spirit will use to bring Jesus' prayer in John 17:21 into glorious fulfillment. As you read this book, ask the Holy Spirit to open and cleanse your mind of anything that would hinder our being *one* in Jesus Christ. Let His perfect love cast out any remaining sin of fear or distrust of fellow-believers in Christ.

We long fervently for Jesus to return for His Bride, but He will not return for a divided, disjointed Body. Let us hasten the glorious return of our Lord Jesus Christ by allowing *love* to cover.

Paul F. Crouch
Founder and President
Trinity Broadcasting Network, Inc.

INTRODUCTION

This book is based upon the same cosmology as *Destined for the Throne* and its sequel, *Don't Waste Your Sorrows*. It affirms that the universe, including this planet, was created to provide a suitable habitation for the human race. The human race was created in the image and likeness of God to provide an Eternal Companion for the Son. After the fall and the promise of redemption, the Messianic race was born and nurtured to bring in the Messiah. The Messiah came for one intent, and only one—to give birth to the Church, thus to obtain His Bride. *Thus the Church becomes the ultimate goal of the universe, and so far as revelation is concerned, the solitary reason for creation.*

In *Destined for the Throne* it is claimed that God designed the system of prayer to equip and qualify the Bride with the techniques, the skills, and the "know-how," administratively or otherwise, for rulership. In *Don't Waste Your Sorrows* it is asserted that God further designed that suffering, which is a consequence of the fall, shall produce the *character* and *disposition,* the *compassionate spirit* which will be required for rulership in a government where the *law of love* is supreme.

When one is born again he immediately enters training for rulership. Because *agape*[1] love, the unconditional love which characterizes God Himself, is an essential qualification for the exercise of authority in the heavenly social order toward which the universe is moving (otherwise called the kingdom of God), therefore, this apprenticeship is for the development of this love. If it were not for the necessity of this training and maturing in love, God probably would take one to heaven as soon as he is saved.

Because tribulation is necessary for the decentralization of self and the development of deep dimensions of agape love, this love can be developed only in the school of suffering. It grows and develops only by exercise and testing. Therefore, following regeneration and the infilling with the Holy Spirit, God places each member of His Bridehood in the place where he or she will develop deeper dimensions of agape love. This love is an essential qualification for rulership in the kingdom of God where the law of love is supreme. *Thus we see that the great business of life is learning agape love.* According to W. E. Vine in his *Expository Dictionary of New Testament Words* (Volume 3, page 20), *agape love* is the love which loves because of its own inherent nature, not because of the excellence or worth of its object. It is the quality of love which originates in, flows from and characterizes God Himself.

In *Don't Waste Your Sorrows,* the part that personal and private relationships play in the development of agape love is considered. In this book, *Love Covers,* the opportunities for growth in love which church, group, or social relationships offer are explored. Many spiritual leaders are convinced that the conflicts encountered in such relationships are crucial in the development of agape love and in accomplishing the unity of His Body.

It is my prayer that you will approach this subject reverently and with an open heart. God longs to see a great enlargement in agape love in His Church universal, not only because of its temporal importance but also because of its eternal importance.

1

LEARNING AGAPE LOVE THROUGH LOCAL CHURCH RELATIONSHIPS

Why God has permitted a proliferation of denominations with their various shades of beliefs has long been a mystery. This is especially puzzling in the light of John 13:34-35 and John 17:20-23. How can the Church justify the divisions, schisms, antagonisms, hostilities and hatreds which have divided the Body of Christ over the centuries?

"A new commandment I give unto you, that ye love one another; as I have loved you, that ye also love one another. By this shall all men know that ye are my disciples, if ye have love one to another" (John 13:34-35).

"Neither pray I for these alone, but for them also who shall believe on me through their word; that they all may be one, as thou, Father, art in me, and I in thee, that they also may be one in us; that the world may believe that thou hast sent me. And the glory which thou gavest me I have given them, that they may be one, even as we are one: I in them, and thou in me, that they may be made perfect in one; and that the world may know that thou hast sent me, and hast loved them, as thou hast loved me." (John 17:20-23).

Not a Criticism of Denominationalism

This book is not a criticism of denominationalism as

such. It seems that Paul tacitly recognized the possibility of denominational differences in Ephesians 4. In verse three he used the phrase "unity of the Spirit," and in verse thirteen, "unity of the faith." The Church is urged to make every effort to maintain the unity of the Spirit in the Body of Christ, which is considered as an organic whole, until the individual members of the Body reach the "unity of the faith, and of the knowledge of the Son of God." This passage regards "faith" and "knowledge" as a body or system of belief sometimes called a theology. The inference is that, although there may be differences of opinion concerning spiritual concepts, those differences should not lead to broken fellowships and division.

The Advantage of Diversity

The following appeared in *The Gospel Herald* on May 4, 1976

A prominent Lutheran theologian says that he has changed his mind about the importance of organic church mergers. Alvin Rogness, President Emeritus of Lutheran Theological Seminary, Saint Paul, Minnesota, says that at one time he was inclined to believe that the union of churches was basic to fulfilling Jesus' prayer, "That they may be one, even as we are one." "I no longer believe that," Rogness wrote in the *Lutheran Standard,* official publication of the American Lutheran Church. "It may be that I was caught up in the American myth that to be bigger was to be better. From simple common sense observation, I know this to be illusory.

"In fact, I have come to believe that the Lord loves diversity, and that only by embracing diversity can we understand the wonder of unity. Just as God has made individual human beings each different from any other, so it may be that the various traditions within His Church are of His making."

Surely this view is worthy of consideration. This could reduce denominational lines mostly to administrative levels.

Unity in Diversity

The Church universal is said to be the Body of Christ. "Just as each one of us has one body with many members, and these members do not all have the same function, so in Christ we who are many form one body, and each member belongs to all the others" (Rom. 12:4-5 *NIV*). "The body is a unit, though it is made up of many parts; and though all its parts are many, they form one body. So it is with Christ....Now you are the body of Christ, and each one of you is a part of it" (1 Cor. 12:12, 27 *NIV*). "God has combined the members of the body and has given greater honor to the parts that lacked it, so that there should be no division in the body" (1 Cor. 12:24-25 *NIV*).

Born-again People Constitute the Body

All truly born-again people are members of the Body. What is the biblical meaning of the new birth? Many of the cults, including Jehovah's Witnesses, New Thought, and various Oriental religions, profess to believe in a new birth. What is the biblical meaning of this term? Scriptural new birth begins in repentance. See Matthew 3:1-12, 4:17; Mark 1:4, 15; Luke 3:3, 24:47.

The Meaning of Repentance and the New Birth

What is the meaning of repentance? According to *Webster's New World Dictionary,* repentance "implies full realization of one's sins or wrongs and a will to change one's ways." Therefore, biblical repentance includes a conviction of sin with a sense of condemnation, godly sorrow for sin, forsaking of sin, restitution for sin. If a person is truly sorry for his sins, he will be willing to make all wrongs right as far as that is possible.

When a person has truly repented, faith for forgiveness comes naturally and the soul is reconciled to God and experiences regeneration which is the new birth.

God Extends Fellowship to Believers

Since all born-again people are members of the Body of Christ, God extends fellowship to them regardless of their position on doctrines not necessary or directly related to the conversion experience. Since this is true, do we have the right to refuse fellowship to other believers when God Himself extends fellowship to them? In doing this, aren't we in danger of diminishing or breaking fellowship with God Himself?

The Basis of Fellowship—Life, Not Opinion

It is clear that God fellowships with people on opposite sides of various disputed doctrines. This suggests that, in God's book, fellowship should be on the basis of life rather than doctrine. I know of no other possible ground for universal unity except a common life, an authentic family relationship. All born-again people have the same Father. No amount of grace will ever enable all born-again people to agree on what formulated doctrinal system constitutes absolute conceptual truth. If the prayer of Jesus for unity of the Body is realized this side of heaven, it will have to be on the basis of a common Fatherhood and that means on the basis of *agape love*. It means that love for the family will exceed devotion to one's personal opinions in non-essentials to salvation. The principles advanced in this paragraph are basic to all that follows. All subsequent positions are predicated upon the acceptance of these concepts. In my opinion, all readers are obligated to accept these premises unless they have a viable alternative.

Fellowship More Important Than Absolutely Correct Theology

This is not a call to compromise sincere convictions. You are not compelled to surrender personal convictions in order to love a brother, a member of the same family circle, who has the same Father. The most vital and tangible cornerstone and foundation of love—and therefore of unity and fellowship—is an ancestral or family relationship rather than a common opinion. If this is true, then fellowship on that basis is more important to God than absolutely correct theology. *God is more interested in love between members of His family than in the inerrancy of one's opinions.* While the Word is inerrant, no one's opinion of a moot or debatable point is. There is a possibility of error in all extra-scriptural doctrinal statements, or any statement of Biblical interpretation. Only the Scripture itself in its original autographs is inerrant. Therefore, no church creed is infallible. Where born-again people are on opposite sides of a question not actually necessary to salvation, agape love should prevent a break in fellowship, or outright division. Such instances offer the opportunity for growth in love and therefore in *eternal rank*. It is a waste of sorrow to permit differences of opinion on beliefs not essential for conversion to produce broken fellowships with their attendant heartaches and pains.

What we say here against division within the Body is in no way contradictory to what Paul wrote to the Corinthian believers in his second epistle. There he is speaking against having spiritual fellowship with "unbelievers," those in "darkness," "infidels." "Be ye not unequally yoked together with unbelievers; for what fellowship hath righteousness with unrighteousness? And what communion hath light with darkness? And what concord hath Christ with Belial? Or what part hath he that believeth with an infidel? And what agreement hath the temple of God with idols? For ye are the temple of the living God; as God hath said, I will dwell in them, and walk in them; and I will be their God, and they shall be my people. Wherefore, come out from among them, and be ye separate, saith the Lord, and touch not the unclean thing; and I will receive you, and will be a Father unto you, and ye shall be my sons and daughters, saith the Lord Almighty." (2 Cor. 6:14-18). This command is in agreement with Deuteronomy 7:1-6, Isaiah 52:11, and Amos 3:3. But breaking fellowship with those who are in the family of God is a completely different matter.

The Greatest Sin of the Church—Disunity

Disunity in the Body of Christ is the scandal of the ages. The greatest sin of the Church is not lying, stealing, drunkenness, adultery—not even murder—but the sin of *disunity*. Because disunity in the Body is more prevalent than these other sins and just as truly ties the hands of the Holy Spirit, it causes more souls to be lost than these flagrant offenses. The Holy Spirit cannot deal effectively in the conviction and conversion of sinners where the "saints" are divided.

Damage on the Mission Field

Perhaps the most atrocious damage of disunity is displayed on the foreign mission field. When missions and missionaries, all claiming to represent Jesus and the gospel, manifest antagonism and hostility to one another, Satan alone is the winner. When inquirers and newly converted believers discover that professed followers of Jesus are fragmented, envious, and even belligerent in spirit, they are often totally devastated. To see the Body of Christ rent by proselytism, greed and jealousy is to them incomprehensible, inexplicable, and even unspeakable. It leaves the national believer totally confused, disillusioned and undone. Perhaps nothing brings greater grief to the heart of the Master than the disgrace of disunity on the mission field.

"Don't Criticize Each Other Any More" (Romans 14:13 *LB*)

Unjust and unloving criticism of one another has been called the "peculiar sin of the saints." In fact, it is the most glaring vice of "holy people." Many who are most emphatic in condemning the doctrine of a sinning religion are most guilty of violating Christ's unequivocal command, "Judge not." This violation is sin.

Christ's command is further emphasized by Paul in Romans chapter 14. He advises the Church on how to deal with a divisive question. "Give a warm welcome to any brother who wants to join you, even though his faith is weak. Don't criticize him for having different ideas from yours about what is right and wrong. For instance, don't argue with him about whether to eat meat that has been offered to idols. You may believe there is no harm in this, but the faith of others is weaker; they think it is wrong....Those who think it is all right to eat such meat must not look down on those who won't. And if you are one of those who won't, don't find fault with those who do. For God has accepted them to be His children. They are God's servants, not yours. They are responsible to him, not to you. Let him tell them whether they are right or wrong. And God is able to make them do as they should. ...You have no right to criticize your brother or look down on him. Remember, each of us will stand personally before the Judgment Seat of God....So don't criticize each other any more" (Rom. 14:1-4,10,13 *LB*).

The Greatest Offenders

For some reason, "saints" who sincerely abhor the sins of lying, stealing and adultery, and who are loudest in their claims to live without sin, are often most guilty of gross disobedience to Christ's positive command and Paul's inspired advice. According to Jesus and Paul, *sitting in judgment upon one another in non-essential matters is sin*. Those groups who major upon the necessity of living above sin are frequently the most glaring trespassers in this area. Those congregations and denominations who preach the highest standard of holiness seem to be the most fragmented.

Unsanctified Ego

Judgmentalism results in the rejection of another born-again brother because of his opinion in matters not essential to salvation. Increasing judgmentalism, therefore, is a sign of decreasing grace. It means we do not believe God knows how or is capable of correcting His children. In other words, it is "playing" God. I admit, with sorrow, that I was guilty of this sin. The average critic has more confidence in criticism than in prayer to remedy a situation. Much of the criticism which leads to disagreements and divisions is not primarily because of superior convictions but because of unsanctified ego and uncrucified flesh. It often betrays a "rule or ruin" syndrome. This was the cause of Satan's fall. It is something to be avoided like the plague that it is. *Most unkind criticism is not because of surpassing spiritual judgment but because of personal frustration and a sense of inferiority*. Those who are being truly fruitful are sufficiently fulfilled to resist the temptation to judge. They do not need to nourish their ego by demeaning others.

The Local Church a Workshop

The Church is considered as a family. "Now, therefore, ye are no more strangers and foreigners, but fellow citizens with the saints, *and of the household of God"* (Eph. 2:19). The local church, therefore, may be viewed as a spiritual workshop for the development of agape love. Thus the stresses and strains of a spiritual fellowship offer the ideal situation for the testing and maturing of the all-important qualification for sovereignty. *It is not as important, in any controversy, that the wisest decisions be made, either practically or doctrinally, as it is that the right spirit be maintained.* Love, like other graces of the Spirit, grows only under testing. Differences of opinion in local church groups offer opportunities to grow in agape love and hence in eternal reward. Divisions over doctrine not dealing with the actual new birth experience, such as policy, polity, or personalities, are *a waste of sorrows* and a grief to the Holy Spirit.

The Best Laboratory

Most controversies in local congregations are produced, not primarily by differences over essentials, but by unsanctified human ambitions, jealousy, and personality clashes. The real root of many such situations is spiritual dearth in individual believers, revealing lamentable immaturity in love. Therefore the local congregation is one of the very best laboratories in which individual believers may discover their real spiritual emptiness and begin to grow in agape love. This is done by true repentance, humbly confessing the sins of jealousy, envy, resentment, etc., and begging forgiveness from one another. This approach will result in real growth in *the love that covers*. It will release the Holy Spirit to heal wounds and quicken revival fires. This is why the Apostle Paul exhorts the Ephesian church to "keep the unity of the Spirit in the bond of peace," noting that there is "one body, one Spirit,...one Lord, one faith, one baptism, one God and Father of all, who is...in you all" (Eph. 4:3-6). Therefore, nothing short of heresy or open sin, which affects relationship with the Father, should be permitted to bring schism in the professed Body of Christ.

2

LEARNING AGAPE LOVE THROUGH DIFFERENCES IN STANDARDS IN EXTERNALS AND PRACTICE

One controversial matter which divides born-again believers is differences in standards in externals and practice. On one side are those who insist on a strict separation from the customs of the world as typified and practiced by Hollywood. They strongly emphasize such passages as Romans 12:2, "And be not conformed to this world, but be ye transformed by the renewing of your mind...." The Phillips rendition may be more pointed: "Don't let the world around you squeeze you into its own mold."

1 Timothy 2:9-10 is another relevant passage. "In like manner, also, that women adorn themselves in modest apparel, with godly fear and sobriety, not with braided hair, or gold, or pearls, or costly array, but (which becometh women professing godliness) with good works." According to Phillips this passage reads, "The women should be dressed quietly, and their demeanor should be modest and serious. The adornment of Christian women is not a matter of elaborate coiffure, expensive clothes or valuable jewelry, but the living of a good life." In the *Living Bible* this passage reads, "And the women should be the same way, quiet and sensible in manner and clothing. Christian women should be noticed for being kind and good,

not for the way they fix their hair or because of their jewels and fancy clothes." Moffatt renders this passage, "Women in turn ought to dress modestly and quietly in seemly garb; they are not to adorn themselves with plaits of hair, with gold or pearls or expensive finery, but with good deeds (as befits women who make a religious profession)." Turning to the *New English Bible,* the passage reads, "Women again must dress in a becoming manner, modestly and soberly, not with elaborate hair-styles, not decked out with gold or pearls, or expensive clothes, but with good deeds, as befits women who claim to be religious."

Another passage which deals with this subject is 1 Peter 3:3-5: "Whose adorning, let it not be that outward adorning of plaiting the hair, and of wearing of gold, or of the putting on of apparel, but let it be the hidden man of the heart in that which is not corruptible, even the ornament of a meek and quiet spirit, which is in the sight of God of great price. For after this manner in the old time the holy women also, who trusted in God, adorned themselves...." Phillips renders this passage, "Your beauty should not be dependent upon an elaborate coiffure, or the wearing of jewelry or fine clothes, but of the inner personality—the unfading loveliness of a calm and gentle spirit, a thing very precious in the eyes of God. This was the secret of the beauty of the holy women of ancient times...." Moffatt translates it, "You are not to adorn yourselves on the outside with braids of hair and ornaments of gold and changes of dress, but inside, in the heart, with the immortal beauty of a gentle and modest spirit, which in the sight of God is of rare value. It was this way long ago that the holy women who hoped in God adorned themselves." The *New English* translation follows: "Your beauty should reside not in outward adornment—the braiding of the hair, or jewelry, or dress—but in the inmost center of your being, with its imperishable ornament, a gentle, quiet spirit, which is of high value in the sight of God. Thus it was among God's people in days of old...."

These passages speak for themselves. They are neither abstruse nor moot. They need no embellishment, elaboration or amplification. But differences of opinion prevail.

Differences in Standards

There is a segment in the Body which feels that these scriptures proscribe the wearing of jewelry, styles which are in any way suggestive or emphasize sex appeal (such as low necklines, short or mini-skirts, tight sweaters) or any apparel which accentuates or in any way exposes or over-glamorizes the female form.

Those of this persuasion point out that from the beginning of the Church age, Christian culture sought to avoid even a hint of the sensual or unchaste. "But among you there must not be even a hint of sexual immorality, or of any kind of impurity, or of greed, because these are improper for God's holy people" (Eph. 5:3 *NIV*). They also refer to the strict standards of separation sponsored by Wesley and the early Methodists, Finney and his followers, the early Holiness and Pentecostal movements, the Mennonites and others. They say that all of these communions exalted the ideals of other-worldly mindedness.

A Modern Religious Culture

In more modern times a culture has arisen which considers itself Christian and which claims that the strict and inflexible standards outlined above constitute a form of legalism, from which they have been liberated by their understanding of the gospel. In the matter of externals—hair styles, certain amusements—and in their general life-style, they exercise greater liberty. Strongly emphasized other-worldly mindedness is considered irrelevant, outmoded, unnecessary, and of little or no spiritual value. They are convinced that God's people have a right to the best of this world as well as the next. For them, separation from the world does not mean rejection of the Hollywood life-style in externals—hair styles, recreational activities and affluent living. They feel that standards which require strict self-discipline in these areas are intolerable legalism. And to them, legalism is anathema. They believe that their spiritual life excels and is superior to that of those they classify as legalists.

An Emotional Issue

Members of each school of thought find it difficult to fellowship with members of the other group. Many members of each persuasion are openly antagonistic toward one another. This is a very emotional issue, and generates intense indignation and unholy intolerance on both sides.

Since the greatest sin of the church is disunity, and since it is scriptural that fellowship should be on the basis of regeneration rather than opinion, then this sensitive issue may also offer an opportunity for growth in agape love. As with all other controversial viewpoints on nonessentials to salvation, the question is not primarily who is right and who is wrong. The question is not even who is most *nearly* right. The question is: Are we sufficiently mature in agape love to accept as our brothers those whom God has accepted as His sons?

The Bridge Is Agape Love

The differences that cannot be bridged by intellectual agreement offer an opportunity to learn a deeper dimension of agape love and enhance eternal rank. The schism in the Body produced by broken fellowship is far more damaging, and therefore is a greater sin than the supposed errors that keep the segments of the Body apart. Increased love is the remedy.

"And now I am no more in the world, but these are in the world, and I come to thee. Holy Father, keep through thine own name those whom thou hast given me, that they may be one, as we are.... That they all may be one, as thou, Father, art in me, and I in thee, that they also may be one in us; that the world may believe that thou hast sent me. And the glory which thou gavest me I have given them, that they may be one, even as we are one: I in them, and thou in me, that they may be made perfect in one; and that the world may know that thou hast sent me and hast loved them, as thou hast loved me" (John 17:11, 21-23).

"So we, being many, are one body in Christ, and every one members one of another" (Rom. 12:5).

"For we being many are one bread, and one body; for we are all partakers of that one bread" (1 Cor. 10:17).

"For as the body is one, and hath many members, and all members of that one body, being many, are one body, so also is Christ. For by one Spirit were we all baptized into one body, whether we be Jews or Gentiles, whether we be bond or free; and have been all made to drink into one Spirit. For the body is not one member, but many....But now are they many members, yet but one body. And the eye cannot say unto the hand, I have no need of thee; nor again the head to the feet, I have no need of you. Nay, much more those members of the body which seem to be more feeble, are necessary: and those members of the body which we think to be less honorable, upon these we bestow more abundant honor; and our uncomely parts have more abundant comeliness. For our comely parts have no need; but God hath tempered the body together, having given more abundant honor to that part which lacked, that there should be no schism in the body, but that the members should have the same care one for another" (1 Cor. 12:12-14, 20-25).

If we understand the Word of God, schism and broken fellowship over incidental doctrines are not only sins, but heinous sins. Stresses over standards in externals offer an opportunity to grow in love and therefore in heavenly rank. *No one needs to compromise his personal conviction or position in order to exercise agape love.*

3

LEARNING AGAPE LOVE THROUGH DENOMINATIONAL AND DOCTRINAL DIFFERENCES

The Calvinist and Arminian Problem

Is it possible for the principle of *agape love* to apply across denominational and doctrinal lines? The lack of it is responsible for the conflicts that have rent the Body of Christ for a long time. *Competition is said to be the life of trade, but in ecclesiastical affairs it can be the death of love.* And that means the loss of eternal rank.

Since disunity in the Body probably sends more people to hell than open sin, breaking fellowship over differences in those standards or practices which are not actually necessary to salvation is a greater sin than the supposed error which precipitated the breach. This is not to claim that honest difference of opinion is wrong. What is wrong is the deficiency in love which allows the difference to divide. Where love is sufficiently the aim or goal, "unity in the Spirit" may be maintained.

Both May Be Born-again

There are born-again people who are Calvinists and there are born-again people who are Arminians. *Does any informed person challenge this statement?* Yet much hostility prevails between members of these theological camps. Both sides are equally guilty, for in each camp there are people who refuse to fellowship with those in the opposite camp. Thus they produce a breach in the Body. This is the figurative equivalent to severing a finger, hand or arm from a body.

The following paragraph, excerpted from *The Prairie Overcomer,* appeared in the August 13, 1949 issue of *Christ for Soul and Body,* official organ of the Anderson Gospel Tabernacle, edited by Paul E. Billheimer. It is submitted here for prayerful consideration by both Calvinists and Arminians.

The Wesleys and the Calvinistic Controversy

Mr. George Whitefield and the Wesleys represented divergent schools of thought. Mr. Whitefield was a glowing evangelist and an ardent Calvinist. The Wesleys, on the other hand, represented the Arminian school of thought. In their early days of zeal and immaturity of spiritual development, they clashed again and again. Whitefield stood stoutly and consistently for Calvin's doctrine of sovereign election and particular redemption. The Wesleys swung to the opposite pole. Later in life, after much growth in grace, the two parties came nearer together.

Do We Out-Wesley Wesley?

I have long taken the position that extreme Calvinism and extreme Arminianism are equally objectionable. It is my firm conviction that the Scriptures lend some support to both points of view. I also believe that there is something in Calvinism which Arminians need ...and vice versa. Today, in certain Arminian circles, such statements as this constitute rank heresy. In the extreme wings of each school, any attempt to fellowship with those of the opposite persuasion is considered as a dangerous compromise. Since I am affiliated with the Arminian school, I will not undertake to confess for nor to correct the Calvinists who may be guilty of this lack of Christian charity. That is a matter for the members of their own household to consider. But I do wish to point out that some of us in the Arminian school are in danger of going to such extremes as to out-Wesley Wesley.

As proof of this fact I offer the following poem by Charles Wesley, printed in a recent issue of *The Prairie Overcomer*. Many extreme Arminians who contend so zealously for Wesley's doctrine of entire sanctification would do well to emulate the humble spirit of acknowledgment and confession which controlled the men who were the originators of the doctrine for which they contend. Many today feel that acknowledgment of one's wrong state of mind is entirely out of harmony with the doctrine of sanctification and therefore incompatible with the experience. I would like to point out the utter frankness of Charles Wesley in acknowledging, in this poem, a rash spirit and other manifestations of the flesh. Take, for instance, such lines as "Too long, alas! we gave to Satan place," and "Rash nature waved the controversial sword." Also, "Fraternal love from every breast was driven, and bleeding charity return'd to heaven." Note in the fifth stanza his plea to disregard differences of opinion and unite against a common foe.

The eleventh stanza is an historical account of the

early fellowship of Whitefield and the Wesleys. It
alludes to their cooperation in America, to which
Whitefield came in response to an invitation by the
Wesleys. The entire poem will bear close study. It
offers an inspired formula for solving many current
problems in other areas of dissension. I especially commend it to my brother ministers, and pray that it may
speak to them as it has to me.

An Epistle to the Reverend
Mr. George Whitefield

Come on, my Whitefield! (Since the strife is
    past,
And friends at first are friends again at last)
Our hands, and hearts, and counsels let us join
In mutual league, t' advance the work Divine,
Our one contention now, our single aim,
To pluck poor souls as brands out of the flame;
To spread the victory of that bloody Cross,
And gasp our latest breath in the Redeemer's
    cause.

Too long, alas!—we gave to Satan place,
When party zeal put on an angel's face:
Too long we listen'd to the deceiving fiend,
Whose trumpet sounded—"For the faith
    contend!"
With hasty blindfold rage in error's night,
How did we with our fellow soldiers fight!
We could not then our Father's children know,
But each mistook his brother for his foe.

"Foes to the truth, can you in conscience spare?
Tear them," the Tempter cried, "in pieces tear!"
So thick the darkness, so confused the noise,
We took the stranger's for the Shepherd's voice;
Rash nature waved the controversial sword,
On fire to fight the battles of the Lord;
Fraternal love from every breast was driven,
And bleeding charity return'd to Heaven.

The Saviour saw our strife with pitying eye,
And cast a look that made the shadows fly;
Soon as the day-spring in His presence shone,
We found the two fierce armies were but one;
Common our hope, and family, and name,
Our arms, our Captain, and our crown the
    same;
Enlisted all beneath Immanuel's sign,
And purchased every soul with blood Divine.

Then let us cordially again embrace,
Nor e'er infringe the league of gospel grace;
Let us in Jesus' name to battle go,
And turn our arms against the common foe;
Fight side by side beneath our Captain's eye,
Chase the Philistines, on their shoulders fly,
And, more than conquerors, in the harness die.

For whether I am born to "blush above,"
On earth suspicious of electing love,
Or you, o'erwhelm'd with honorable shame,
To shout the universal Saviour's name,
It matters not; if, all our conflicts past,
Before the great white throne we meet at last:

Our only care, while sojourning below,
Our real faith by real love to show.

To blast the alien's hope and let them see
How friends of jarring sentiments agree:
Not in a party's narrow banks confined,
Not by a sameness of opinions join'd,
But cemented with the Redeemer's blood.
And bound together in the heart of God.

Can we forget from whence our union came,
When first we simply met in Jesus' name?
The name mysterious of the GOD UNKNOWN,
Whose secret love allured, and drew us on
Through a long, lonely, legal wilderness,
To find the promised land of gospel peace.

True yokefellows, we then agreed to draw
Th' intolerable burden of the law;
And jointly laboring on with zealous strife,
Strength'nd each other's hands to work for
    life;
To turn against the world our steady face,
And, valiant for the truth, enjoy disgrace.

Then, when we served our God through fear
    alone,
Our views, our studies, and our hearts were
    one;
No smallest difference damp'd the social
    flame:
In Moses' school we thought, and spake the
    same:
And must we, now in Christ, with shame
    confess,

Our love was greater when our light was less?
When darkly through a glass with servile awe,
We first the spiritual commandment saw,
Could we not then, our mutual love to show,
Through fire and water for each other go?

We could: we did. In a strange land I stood,
And beckon'd thee to cross th' Atlantic flood:
With true affection winged, thy ready mind
Left country, fame, and ease, and friends
    behind;
And, eager all Heaven's counsels to explore,
Flew through the watery world and grasp'd
    the shore.

Nor did I linger, at my friend's desire,
To tempt the furnace, and abide the fire:
When, suddenly sent forth, from the highways
I call'd poor outcasts to the feast of grace;
Urged to pursue the work by thee begun,
Through good and ill report I still rush'd on,
Nor felt the fire of popular applause,
Nor fear'd the torturing flame in such a
    glorious cause.

Ah! Wherefore did we ever seem to part,
Or clash in sentiment, while one in heart?
What dire device did the old Serpent find,
To put asunder those whom God had join'd?
From folly and self love, opinion rose
To sever friends who never yet were foes;
To baffle and divert our noblest aim,
Confound our pride, and cover us with
    shame.

To make us blush beneath her short-lived
  power,
And glad the world with one triumphant
  hour.

But lo! The snare is broke, the captive's
  freed,
By faith on all the hostile powers we tread,
And crush through Jesus' strength the
  Serpent's head.
Jesus hath cast the cursed Accuser down,
Hath rooted up the tares by Satan sown:
Kindled anew the never dying flame,
And re-baptized our souls into His name.

Soon as the virtue of His name we feel,
The storm of strife subsides, the sea is still,
All nature bows to His benign command,
And two are one in His almighty hand.

One in His hand, O may we still remain,
Fast bound with love's indissoluable chain;
That adamant which time and death defies,
That golden chain which draws us to the
  skies!
His love the tie that binds us to His throne,
His love the bond that perfects us in one;
His love, let all the ground of friendship see,
His only love constrains our hearts t'agree,
And gives the rivet of eternity.

An Antinomy
The apparent irreconcilability between Calvinism

and Arminianism is called an antinomy by J. I. Packer, a leading exponent of the Calvinistic viewpoint. He defines an antinomy as an apparent incompatibility between two apparent truths. "An antinomy exists when a pair of principles stand side by side, seemingly irreconcilable, yet both undeniable. There are cogent reasons for believing each of them; each rests on clear and solid evidence; but it is a mystery to you how they can be squared with each other. You see that each must be true on its own, but cannot see how they can both be true together. Let me give an example. Modern physics faces an antinomy, in this sense, in its study of light. There is cogent evidence to show that light consists of waves, and equally cogent evidence to show that it consists of particles. It is not apparent how light can be both waves and particles, but the evidence is there, and so neither view can be ruled out in favour of the other. Neither, however, can be reduced to the other or explained in terms of the other; the two seemingly incompatible positions must be held together, and both be treated as true." [2]

God's Responsibility

Dr. Packer sees an antinomy in the doctrines of divine sovereignty and human responsibility. He suggests that both are biblical and that both should be accepted and believed. Although apparently irreconcilable, neither should be allowed to obscure or overshadow the other. If I understand Dr. Packer, he suggests that where the Bible supports the Calvinistic viewpoint, it should be accepted. Where it supports the Arminian viewpoint, it should also be accepted. It is not man's responsibility to harmonize these apparent opposites. It is God's.

A Question of Semantics

In 2 Timothy 2:14, 23-25 Paul warns against unnecessary controversy. He says, "Warn them before God against quarreling about words; it is of no value and only ruins those who listen.... Don't have anything to do with foolish and stupid arguments, because you know they produce quarrels. And the Lord's servant must not quarrel; instead, he must be kind to everyone, able to teach, not resentful. Those who oppose him he must gently instruct" (*NIV*).

Much of the difference between Calvinists and Arminians seems purely semantic. Someone has said that Calvinists call their mistakes sins while Arminians call all of their sins mistakes. In the preceding poem, Charles Wesley openly acknowledged that the broken fellowship between the Wesleys and Whitefield had its roots in unlovingness more than in zeal for doctrinal purity. Since fellowship should be on the basis of *life* rather than *doctrinal correctness,* then shouldn't Calvinists and Arminians bury their theological hatchets?

A Dialogue With Wesley

Charles Simeon, a leading Calvinist of Wesley's day, did just that following a dialogue with John Wesley. The account of this confrontation is recorded on pages thirteen and fourteen of *Evangelism and the Sovereignty of God* by Dr. Packer.

It is instructive in this connection to ponder Charles Simeon's account of his conversation with John Wesley on December 20th, 1784 (the date is given in Wesley's *Journal*): ' "Sir, I understand that you are called an Arminian; and I have been sometimes called a Calvinist; and therefore I suppose we are to draw daggers. But before I consent to begin the combat, with your permission I will ask you a few questions....Pray, Sir, do you feel yourself a depraved creature, so depraved that you would never have thought of turning to God, if God had not first put it into your heart?" "Yes," says the veteran, "I do indeed." "And do you utterly despair of recommending yourself to God by anything you can do; and look for salvation solely through the blood and righteousness of Christ?" "Yes, solely through Christ." "But, Sir, supposing you were at first saved by Christ, are you not somehow or other to save yourself afterwards by your own works?" "No, I must be saved by Christ from first to last." "Allowing, then, that you were first turned by the grace of God, are you not in some way or other to keep yourself by your own power?" "No." "What, then, are you to be upheld every hour and every moment by God, as much as an infant in its mother's arms?" "Yes, altogether." "And is all your hope in the grace and mercy of God to preserve you unto His heavenly kingdom?" "Yes, I have no hope but in Him." "Then, Sir, with your leave I will put up my dagger again; for this is all my Calvinism; this is my election, my justification by faith, my final perseverance: it is in substance all that I hold, and as I hold it; and therefore, if you please, instead of searching out terms and phrases to be a ground of contention between us, we will cordially unite in those things wherein we agree." '

Peter says, "Above all things have fervent love among yourselves, for love shall cover the multitude of sins" (1 Peter 4:8, *New Scofield Bible*). Since love covers a multitude of sins, shouldn't it also cover honest differences between Calvinists and Arminians today, just as it did in Wesley's and Simeon's day? Yielding to the temptation to indulge in "foolish and stupid arguments" that produce quarrels (2 Tim. 2:23 *NIV*) *is a waste of sorrows.* Won't we learn agape love by following the example of the Wesleys and Charles Simeon and "bury our hatchets" and "put up our daggers" and "cordially unite in those things wherein we agree," instead of wounding the Body of Christ?

After all, the most important question is not who is right or who is wrong—not even who is most nearly right. The important question is: What are we most interested in—proving our point and promoting our own theological concept, thus saving our theological face? Or do we desire to be the answer to Christ's prayer for unity by healing the wounds of His body, and making possible the outpouring of His Spirit on a world-wide scale. To understand and unite in those things wherein we agree will narrow the gap between contending viewpoints of nonessentials to salvation. But *agape love,* love for Jesus Himself and genuine sympathy for His longing for unity, will discard it completely. It will heal the breach, make His Body whole, and bring joy to His aching heart.

4

LEARNING AGAPE LOVE THROUGH DIFFERENCES ON THE WORK OF THE HOLY SPIRIT

The Charismatic Movement

Another controversial issue that offers an opportunity for the exercise of agape love to prevent schism in the Body of Christ is the current Charismatic movement. It seems ironic that among those displaying the most violent opposition and implacable hostility to this movement are adherents of the so-called Holiness movement. These trace their ancestry to the Wesleyan emphasis on the work of the Holy Spirit. In fact, the Pentecostal movement is considered by some as a kind of stepchild, or at least a first cousin, of the Wesleyan fellowship. Its invasion today of the old-line denominations, including the liturgical confessions, especially the Roman Church, is as phenomenal as its rejection by the Holiness groups.

A Surprising Anomaly

How does accepting the "body truth" Paul taught concerning the Church, and the position that fellowship should be on the basis of *regeneration* rather than *doctrine,* affect the relationship between Charismatics and non-Charismatics? Since the beginning of the Pentecostal movement around the turn of the century, association with it has meant you were stigmatized, ostracized, and rejected by non-Pentecostals. To be identified with tongues in any way was the epitome of disgrace. Attending a Pentecostal meeting was reason enough to be scandalized.

Today that is rapidly changing. But there are many in the old-line denominations, and especially in the Holiness persuasion, who still have reservations. The Charismatic renewal is penetrating the affiliations that have historically flatly rejected the Wesleyan doctrine of a second work of grace. On the other hand, the denominational groups that have been built upon that doctrine are most adamant in their opposition to the Charismatics—although they major on "baptism with the Holy Spirit" as an experience subsequent to regeneration. To many, this is an anomaly.

All Sin Is Against Love

It is understandable that there might be differences of opinion on the distinctive doctrines held by Pentecostals. The widespread rejection of the doctrine that speaking in tongues is the initial evidence of the "baptism" or filling with the Holy Spirit is explainable. But open hostility is not excusable, because it is the direct result of imperfect love. If this is true, isn't it enough to make angels weep? *All sin is against love. There is no sin that is not a violation of love.* Where does this place those who so powerfully preach against a sinning relgion and yet continue to sin against love by refusing to fellowship with members of the Body who are Pentecostals?

A Prudent Approach

While the Holiness movement continues its adamantine opposition to the Charismatic renewal, denominations which have historically rejected the Wesleyan teaching on the second work of grace are being influenced by that concept as sponsored by the Charismatics.

One of those denominations is the Old Mennonites. Emphasis on a second work of grace has never been an accepted part of their theology. Yet when the Charismatic movement began to penetrate their ranks, did they wave a red flag and cry, "Fanaticism"? No! Instead, the church leaders themselves seized the initiative. Since the reviving work of the Holy Spirit had been felt and manifested early on the campuses of their educational institutions, they led the way by officially sponsoring what they called "A Festival of the Holy Spirit." They invited as their principal speakers some leading exponents of the renewal. The speakers included one of their own lifelong missionaries who had recently received the "baptism with the Holy Spirit" in a conference at Notre Dame.

An Illustration

An extract from an editorial by John M. Drescher, in *The Gospel Herald,* official organ of the Old Mennonite Church, is presented here as an illustration.

Many places I have gone in the past few years people have asked me what I think of the Charismatic movement. My answer is that the Charismatic movement has brought new life to the church, and, except for those few places where it seems to be divisive (every movement has certain extremes), it is a good thing for the church. Persons I know who are involved love Christ and the church more, study the Scriptures with a new seriousness, and have found a new freedom and fervor in witness to Christ.

My answer is that the Charismatic movement cannot be considered peripheral to the life of the church. It cuts across denominational lines and it is clear that every economic, social, educational, and religious group has significant representation in the group. The movement is predominantly lay in character, yet it is not anti-clergy. In fact, ministers and the church as a whole will find the biggest resource available today in those involved in the Charismatic movement.

It is clear that the Charismatic movement will not go away. And let us pray it will not. No movement in modern times has so vitalized the life of the church in prayer, praise, and serious Bible study as this movement. Who can deny that prayer and praise and love of the Word flow from the greater fullness of the Spirit? The movement has to do with the fullness of life in the Holy Spirit—and how we need this emphasis!

Though the Charismatic is not strong generally in biblical exegesis or systematic theology, yet he has grasped the core of the gospel with refreshing accuracy. There is a new freedom of the Spirit not only in witness, but also in ways of worshipping, expectation, and manner of evangelism. Most denominations and congregations carry a lot of cultural baggage, in worship, work and witness, which needs to be challenged.

We ought to have deep appreciation for those who are involved in the Charismatic movement. It is doubtful if any other part of the church will bring to the church any greater resources in prayer, Bible study, and witness. And every congregation which seeks revival can, I believe, find a committed core made up mostly today of those who have experienced a renewed openness to the filling with the Holy Spirit.

As in every movement, there are areas of danger —and we must continually bring our experience to the test of Scripture. (Certainly our past experience of dryness, lukewarmness, and ineffective witness would not correspond to Scripture.) We must recognize that, in any area, we can miss the real meaning and the experience God is just waiting to give, by a fearful weighing and preoccupation with every danger.

What the church needs is a spiritual renewal of love for Christ and His people, of love for the Scripture and obedience to it, of openness and obedience to the Holy Spirit, and of effective witness to the world. In all of these, I feel, the Charismatic movement has done much in leading the way (*Gospel Herald,* August 7, 1973).

Pentecostalism a Protest Movement

In his excellent little book *Tongues, Psychic and Authentic,* Dr. David A. Seamonds quotes Dr. George R. Failing, editor of the *Wesleyan Advocate.* He is quoted as saying, "Pentecostalism is the protest movement of our day. It is a protest against the coldness of the Holiness denominations."

If this is correct, wouldn't it be more logical and more in the authentic spirit of agape love if we joined in thanking the Pentecostals for emphasizing the ministry of the Holy Spirit which originally was the genius of the Wesleyan movement? Shouldn't this give pause to the opposition by the Wesleyan school of theology to the movement which allegedly has helped restore, at least partially, the vitality and spontaneity of the early Wesleyan revival?

Endorsement by a Leader of the Wesleyan Persuasion

The position of most Holiness denominations is tantamount to forbidding to speak in tongues. In spite of this, one leader prominent in the movement has recently acknowledged that speaking in tongues is a bona fide gift of the Spirit for today. Dr. David A. Seamonds, mentioned above, is pastor of the United Methodist Church of Wilmore, Kentucky, the host church of Asbury College and Seminary. In his book Dr. Seamonds clearly states that he believes there is an authentic gift of tongues, entirely distinct from the foreign languages spoken in Acts 2:7-8. While he argues that the Pentecostals err by disproportionately emphasizing the gift of tongues, he refers to "many others at the other extreme who are just as wrong in failing to seek the gifts of the Spirit and being willing to accept whatever gift He may choose to give" (page 26). He refers to "those who unbiblically oppose all tongues and the Charismatic movement in general" (page 25).

Although he recognizes a grave lack of balance in certain areas among Pentecostals, he says, "Personally,

I am so grateful for what the Spirit is doing through the present-day Charismatic movement that I want to see it stay alive with increasing creativity and vitality" (pages 27-28).

Danger of Imbalance

Dr. Seamonds' position is in contrast with that of most leaders in the Holiness movement. Hopefully he has opened the way for an accommodation between the Charismatic and Holiness communions. It seems there is responsibility on *both* sides for the cleavage which exists. Dr. Seamonds has pointed out one reason for cleavage on the Charismatic side. He says, "Many Charismatics, particularly in the early stages of their joyous experience, tend to overrate the gift of tongues and get it all out of proportion to the other more important gifts of the Spirit. Then they tend to become *spiritual prima donnas* [emphasis mine], upstaging everyone else and forgetting that they are but one member of the cast." Charismatics might serve their own cause and the cause of Christ better if they noted this criticism and avoided this error.

Renewal in Methodism

One of the most surprising and significant developments was reported in the *Atlanta Constitution* of December 6, 1975, under the headline, "One-hundred and Fifty Ministers Receive the Baptism of the Holy Spirit." The account reveals that "almost a hundred and fifty United Methodist ministers received the baptism of the Holy Spirit in a prayer meeting in Atlanta Thursday night, with a large number of the ministers speaking in tongues."

The prayer session came at the close of the first of a three-day Conference on the Holy Spirit for United Methodist Ministers.... During a ten-minute prayer period, the majority of the ministers present prayed aloud, many of them speaking in unknown tongues.

Other ministers speaking to the Conference praised the work of the Spirit in main-line denominations today and called for a church-wide charismatic renewal.

The Rev. Charles Bolyn, pastor of the Oak Grove United Methodist Church in Atlanta, cited the need for a charismatic renewal in the Methodist Church, and said the movement was in keeping with John Wesley's theology....

"John Wesley (the founder of Methodism) would have been right at home with the modern charismatic movement," Bolyn said. "What God is doing in the church today with the baptism of the Holy Spirit is the same thing Wesley was talking about," he said.

The Holiness movement originally came out of the Methodist Church in order to better promote the original Wesleyan emphasis. Most members of this group have long since abandoned ecclesiastical Methodism as irretrievably moribund or even spiritually apostate. In its balmiest days it would have been difficult for the early leaders of the Holiness movement to envision the scene described in this newspaper article.

General Conference Position

More astounding is the position officially taken by

the recent Conference of the United Methodist Church meeting in Portland, Oregon. According to the *Atlanta Constitution* of May 4, 1976, the Conference adopted a lengthy report on the Charismatic movement that calls for "a spirit of openness and of love." The following is a significant passage from the report which conceivably deserves sympathetic consideration by spiritual leaders of other groups who have strong reservations on the movement.

"We are not unmindful that the problems of discrimination between the true and the fraudulent are considerable, but we must not allow the problems to paralyze our awareness of the Spirit's presence; *nor should we permit our fear of the unknown and the unfamiliar to close our mind against being surprised by grace*" (emphasis mine).

The extensive guidelines in the report call for all church members to be "open and accepting" to those whose Christian experiences differ from their own. It also sets up guidelines for both pastors and laity who have had Charismatic experiences.

A Basis for Rapprochement

On the other side of the "wall of partition," some non-Pentecostals have gone to the other extreme. They are forbidding to speak in tongues and soft-pedaling and ignoring the gifts of the Spirit in general. Generally it is understood that if anyone in a Holiness denomination admitted to speaking in tongues *even in his private devotions,* he would probably be disfellowshipped and ostracized. It is difficult not to wonder how these people would feel if the Apostle Paul were to appear today and testify, "I thank God that I speak in tongues more than all of you" (1 Cor. 14:18 *NIV*). It seems that something has gone wrong on both sides which *agape love could correct.* If Pentecostals are in the Body and non-Pentecostals are in the Body, it seems positively imperative to find some ground for rapprochement and rapport. *It is probable that the communion which is closest to God and is most sensitive to the cry of the Master in John 17 will take the initiative in reconciliation and restoration of fellowship.* It is doubtful if all differences of opinion will be resolved this side of heaven. But since *love covers a multitude of sins,* might it not also cover differences of opinion, enabling Pentecostals and non-Pentecostals to learn agape love in the process?

Unity in Diversity

I'm not suggesting that fellowship requires Charismatics and non-Charismatics to worship in the same communion or officially cooperate under the same ecclesiastical umbrella. I am speaking of a spiritual and idealistic, not a formal, organizational ecumenism. But if the Mennonite, United Methodist, Presbyterian, Episcopalian, and many other old-line denominations including the Catholic, find it possible to accomodate the Charismatics with blessing and benefit, may it not be that groups which forbid speaking in tongues are suffering loss? Such groups may be ignoring the principle of unity in diversity expressed by Alvin N. Rogness in Chapter 1. Whether you accept his view or not, it is unmistakably clear that the fragmentation of Christ's Church over nonessentials to salvation is satanic in origin. John Wesley emphasized perfect love as the heart of his message. Is it possible that he intended to exclude those who speak in tongues or those who differed with him on nonessentials? He was known to be generous, large spirited, and tolerant in these areas. Should those who boast of their loyalty to John Wesley's teaching be less magnanimous?

No Movement Perfect

In spite of the discrepancies among them, other credible witnesses believe God is doing something authentic through the Charismatic movement. It has many defects, but so do other fellowships. It is enigmatic, but so are others. It is mingled with error. But no theology is truth absolute, and to forbid to speak with tongues is also error. Some exploit it for selfish purposes. According to the Apostle Paul, the gospel was also exploited in his day (see Philippians 1:15-16; 2 Corinthians 2:17). Pentecostalism is divisive. But many other doctrines have been divisive also.

Do Not Forbid

After all, the most important questions are not those raised above. Are Charismatics, in general, members of the Body? Schism in the Body produces pain and scars in the Church, which is to become His Bride, and His co-regent through eternal ages. To qualify for this task, agape love is essential in one's character. Shouldn't we, as mutual members of His Body, accept our differences not as occasions for broken fellowship but for the development of a strong bond of agape love? Otherwise, we may be reducing our eternal rank and disappointing God. "Beloved, let us love one another, for love is of God" (1 John 4:7). "Therefore, my brothers, be eager to prophesy, and do not forbid speaking in tongues" (1 Cor. 14:39 *NIV*).

To repeat: The real question is not who is right—not even who is most nearly right. The real question is: Do we recognize that God loves and accepts other members of the Body who differ from us in matters nonessential to salvation? Are we sufficiently mature in agape love to accept those whom He accepts? Or are we so egotistic that our opinion in nonessentials is more important to us than unity with God's family and ours? Are we more interested in maintaining our point of view than in helping to bring unity within Christ's Body?

5

QUESTIONS AND ISSUES THAT DIVIDE

A Basic Question of Theology

The real issue that divides Charismatics and non-Charismatics is not primarily tongues. It goes far deeper than that. They are divided over a basic but non-essential question of theology. It revolves around the understanding of Hebrews 13:8, "Jesus Christ, the same yesterday, and today, and forever."

A generation ago Alexander Maclaren, a famous Bible expositor of Manchester, England, articulated a theology on which both Charismatics and non-Charismatics should be able to unite. There are few more highly respected Bible expositors than he. His masterful treatment of Matthew 17:20 is an example.

Concerning the disciples' failure to cast out a demon from a possessed boy, Maclaren wrote: "You will sometimes hear it said, 'God sends forth His Spirit in special fulness at special times according to His sovereign will; and till then we can only wait and pray.' Or, 'the miraculous powers which dwelt in the early Church have been withdrawn and therefore the progress is slow.' " To this he replies:

> The Church has in it a power which is ever adequate to the conquest of the world; and that power is constant through all time....We have a gospel that can never grow old....We have an abiding Spirit, the

Giver to us of a power without variableness or the shadow of turning....We have a Lord, the same yesterday, and today, and forever....The mists of gathering ages wrap in slowly thickening folds of forgetfulness all other men and events in history, and make them ghostlike and shadowy; but no distance has yet dimmed or will ever dim that human form divine. Other names are like those stars that blaze out for a while, and then smoulder down into almost complete invisibility; but He is the very Light itself, that burns and is not consumed. Other landmarks sink below the horizon as the tribes of men pursue their solemn march through the centuries, but the cross of Calvary 'shall stand for an ensign of the people, and to it shall the Gentiles seek.'...A living Saviour in the present, who works with us, confirming the Word with signs following, is the source of our power. Not till He is impotent shall we be weak....He is ever bestowing. He never withdraws what He once gives. The fountain sinks not a hair's-breadth, though nineteen centuries have drawn from it....With such a force at our command ...how can we ever fail?...Nowhere else, in heaven or in earth or in hell, but only in us, lies the reason for our breakdown if we have broken down. Not in God, who is ever with us;...not in the gospel which we preach;...not in the demon might which has overcome us, for 'greater is He that is in us than he that is in the world,'...but only we are to blame.... We have the awful prerogative of limiting the Holy One of Israel....We receive all spiritual gifts in proportion to our capacity, and the chief factor in settling the measure of our capacity is our faith....*In itself the gift is boundless* [emphasis mine].[3]

Can even a non-Charismatic take offense to this eloquent defense of the unchangeableness of Christ and the gospel?

Here is a theology by a pre-Charismatic that should inspire Charismatics and non-Charismatics alike. It should stimulate the faith of both without offending either. It is a theology that, in my opinion, both schools should accept. If both did, there should be no breach of fellowship, regardless of other differences. If a pre-Charismatic can so beautifully articulate a Charismatic theology, why should there be a division between them?

A Question of Literalness

Does God intend for the Church to take Hebrews 13:8 literally; that is, word-for-word according to the original language? Or may it be taken figuratively, or symbolically? Most believers in the inerrancy of the Word hold that all Scripture must be taken literally, word-for-word, as expressed in the original language, unless it is clearly figurative or symbolic. Yet many who accept the inerrancy of the Word differ as to how literally Hebrews 13:8 is to be interpreted and applied.

The First Century Church God's Prototype?

To some, Hebrews 13:8 means that all the power that ever was available to the Church in any age is available today. They believe, as apparently Maclaren did, that God never withdrew anything at any time, and that all loss is due to the Church's unbelief. To some it means that all the miracles recorded in the Bible, of the prophets and apostles and of Jesus Himself, should be normative to the end of the age. These include the equivalent of the opening of the Red Sea and the Jordan River, the supply of manna from heaven, walking on the water, multiplication of the loaves and fishes, healing of leprosy and other diseases, restoration of maimed or broken members of the body, and the raising of the dead. These people are convinced that the first century Church is God's prototype for the entire age. Some have professed to have either exercised or witnessed this miracle-working power in almost every category recorded in Scripture.

An example is the story of the Indonesian revival on the island of Timor in 1965. One published account of the revival told of spectacular healings and even of the dead being brought back to life. Although the authenticity of this report was challenged in certain reliable quarters, its claims are characteristic of the Charismatic movement. Many other miracles, some comparable to those recorded in Scripture, are also allegedly occuring today. One recent instance is the claim of Chinese believers that many miracles similar to those recorded in the New Testament have been observed by the suffering Church in China.

Spiritualizing Miracles

There are others who accept the inerrancy of the Word and who confidently believe Hebrews 13:8, who also believe that at least some of the gifts of the Spirit were officially withdrawn at the close of the Apostolic age. Historically this is the view of Reformed theology and of Dispensationalism. Charismatics believe that the atonement covers the entire scope of human need, spiritual, mental, and material. Some non-Charismatics believe that it is limited to spiritual needs alone. Some few even believe that Jesus' miracles were parables and are to be understood as applying only in the spiritual realm. That is, they "spiritualize" them.

A Moderated View

While the great emphasis in Pentecostalism at large remains on the gift of tongues, a moderating trend seems evident in some significant circles. Without discounting the value of the gift, some highly respected leaders of the movement have abandoned the dogmatic position that the "baptism" or filling with the Holy Spirit is limited to those who speak in tongues. While testifying to the blessing that the gift has brought into their own lives and ministries, they recognize that many of the greatest spiritual leaders in Church history did not speak in tongues. Even though some zealous Pentecostals claim that Luther, for instance, spoke in tongues, there is no evidence that he sponsored the modern Pentecostal emphasis for his followers. Some claim that John Wesley, Charles Finney and Dwight Moody all spoke in tongues. Even if these claims could be documented, which many doubt, none of their followers practiced or promoted this view. Likewise, although members of his staff deny the charge, some Pentecostals persist in spreading the rumor that Billy Graham speaks in tongues in his private devotions.

Some spiritual leaders who are totally committed to the general Pentecostal theology have fully recognized the problem posed by the dogmatic position that only those speaking in tongues have been "baptized" or filled with the Spirit. They recognize the divisive effect of maintaining a superiority complex which dogmatically excludes all those who do not speak in tongues from the Spirit-filled category.

Evidence that speaking in tongues is not universal among Pentecostals (as generally considered) is presented in an astonishing article in the February 22, 1980 issue of *Christianity Today*. Under the title, "The Charismatics Among Us," the article, based upon a Gallup poll, surprisingly reveals that only a small fraction of those who label themselves as Pentecostal-Charismatic actually have spoken in tongues. According to the poll, approximately one-sixth (or roughly five million of the twenty-nine million adult Americans who consider themselves Pentecostal or Charismatic) have spoken in tongues.

This article, written by Kenneth S. Kantzer, editor of *Christianity Today*, alleges that the Gallup poll shows that only one-sixth—seventeen percent—of the Pentecostal-Charismatics speak in tongues. But this was no surprise to Pentecostal-Charismatic leaders. Previous studies have shown that from *fifty percent to sixty-five percent* of church members who accept classical Pentecostal teachings and who are *full members* of a Pentecostal denomination have never spoken in tongues!

Although some Pentecostals challenge the accuracy of these findings, they indicate that speaking in tongues among Pentecostals is not as widely practiced as previously supposed. This raises the question by non-

Charismatics: If these figures are even remotely correct, why should Pentecostals and Charismatics make a distinction by fellowshipping with those who don't speak in tongues *within* the movement more readily than with those *outside* the movement? And why should people outside the movement be so reluctant to fellowship with those within the movement when, according to George Gallup, only a small percentage speak in tongues? Doesn't this indicate that hostility between the groups is unwarranted and Satan-inspired?

6

SEEKING TO HEAL THE BREACH—I

No Viewpoint Intrinsically Divisive

Sometimes it is claimed that the exercise of the gift of tongues is divisive. We should understand that any issue that is controversial is potentially divisive unless it is "handled with love." But it is not the issue itself that produces division. No controversial viewpoint is intrinsically divisive. *All controversy, discord, or division resides, not in the points of dissent or disagreement, but in the parties themselves.* And where nonessentials are concerned, it is all because of a lack of love. All fragmentation or breaking of fellowship, all antagonism occurs *only when there is insufficient love on one side or both.* Breaches in the Body over nonessentials are caused not primarily by error or even by differences of opinion on doubtful questions, but by one thing and one alone: *a lack of agape love. I believe this lack of love is a greater sin in God's sight than the alleged error which triggered the break.*

Equal Responsibility

It may be said that an error in doctrine or a policy over which we differ is injurious to the Body. We claim that is why we break fellowship. *But the injury caused by the alleged error may be less painful, harmful, or destructive than the breach itself which we permitted.* Although those who do not speak in tongues lay the responsibility for division upon the zealousness of those who do, they themselves may also be responsible. *Could it be that the hostility of anti-Charismatics may be as responsible for division as the overemphasis on tongues?* Both probably share some blame.

The Importance of Meekness

One of the things which is offensive to those who do not speak in tongues is the spirit of superiority which they often sense in those who exercise this gift. It is claimed that traces of spiritual pride, sometimes even arrogance, feature their testimonies and their publications. If one is truly superior, that is, superior in God's sight, he will be the last one to feel that way. If he does feel superior, it is conclusive proof that he is not. *True superiority in God's sight is meekness, humility, and brokenness.* The only superiority that God recognizes is that set forth in Philippians chapter 2, where the writer speaks of the humility of Jesus who "made himself of no reputation...and became obedient unto death, even the death of the cross." *The Holy Spirit is the Spirit of meekness* (Gal. 5:22-23). The only One who possessed the Spirit without measure was "meek and lowly in heart" (Matt. 11:29). A spirit of meekness, therefore, should be preeminent in any movement which He controls.

Exaggeration Counterproductive

In the March 26, 1976 issue of *Christianity Today,* Billy Graham is quoted as believing that the Charismatic movement has been used of God to rouse dead Christians in many parts of the world, especially in the main-line denominations. But he is also quoted as believing that there is much in it that is counterfeit. Many other non-Pentecostals are "turned off" by the profuse and apparently exaggerated claims of undocumented miracles and healings that are irresponsibly tossed about in many circles. Sometimes these claims appear to border on dishonesty, and smell of Madison Avenue glamorization of personalities. *Everyone, both Charismatics and non-Charismatics, should remember that it is impossible to glorify Jesus while promoting self or the flesh.*

Sometimes overzealousness in some who speak in tongues seems to lead to preposterous and unsupportable claims that may parade as great faith. Requests for verification and the documentation of such claims may trigger the charge of unbelief. But genuine faith produces such great and glorious results that exaggeration is unnecessary. *Therefore, exaggeration or undocumented reporting is not really a demonstration of faith.* It simply means we think God should have done more than the facts warrant. Exaggerated reports and claims of conversions and healings may strain credibility and actually be counterproductive. Genuine faith does not feel the need to exaggerate.

Documented Miracles

In spite of the foregoing criticism, the conviction is growing that God is performing some works that are uncontestably miraculous even to the most dubious and skeptical minds.

Among those most incredible but undeniable miracles is the healing from multiple myeloma (cancer of the bone) of Rev. Robert Fierro. No more remarkable miracle is recorded among those of Jesus' own ministry upon earth.

For fifty years Robert Fierro has ministered under the auspices of the Assemblies of God. In June of 1974 he became ill and was diagnosed as suffering from multiple myeloma. For nearly five years he was given chemotherapy and/or radiation at the Good Samaritan Hospital in San Jose, California, and the Santa Clara Medical Center, plus much other specialized treatment as complications of various kinds developed. For most of this time he was not only confined to bed or a wheel chair, but was unable to feed or shave himself or even brush his teeth. His pain was so intense that synthetic drugs became ineffective and for many months he required heavy injections of morphine.

In early April of 1979 Mrs. Fierro had a compelling leading that they should return to Puerto Rico where Robert had often ministered with great blessing. They had many loyal, praying friends there.

On April 7, after taking a strong injection of morphine for pain, Rev. Fierro was preaching from his wheel chair when, suddenly, as he was quoting Romans 8:11: "He that raised up Christ from the dead shall also quicken your mortal bodies by his Spirit that dwelleth in you," the mighty healing power of the Holy Spirit caused him to leap from his wheel chair and begin running around the huge stage where he was speaking. This was in the presence of a congregation of 3,000 people. From that day until now, Rev. Fierro has continued in a busy schedule of ministry. One of the remarkable features of his healing was his complete deliverance from the need for morphine with absolutely no withdrawal symptoms.

This remarkable story will soon appear in book form. Full documentation of this "impossible" case is available by an impressive list of highly specialized doctors and the records of two hospitals.

A Second Case

Dr. Richard Eby is well known in his profession as a certified obstetrician and gynecologist. He has served as the President of the Kansas City College of Osteopathy and Surgery and the American College of Osteopathic Obstetricians and Gynecologists.

He was co-founder of the Park Avenue Hospital in Pomona, California, and of the former California Osteopathic Hospital Association. He also served as the Executive Assistant of the American Osteopathic Association in Chicago, and Professor of Obstetrics at the Kirksville College of Osteopathic Medicine. He was the Charter President of the Osteopathic Physicians and Surgeons of California in 1961.

The record of Dr. Eby's accidental death when he fell from a second-story balcony (landing on his head on a jagged block of cement, splitting his skull open), his return to life after being dead for two hours, and his highly visible healing rivals the biblical narrative of the raising of Lazarus.

This story is graphically told in a "best-seller," *Caught Up Into Paradise*.

Another remarkable illustration of the supernatural is the amazing but totally documented account of the extended coma, subsequent death, and resurrection of Mrs. Betty Malz. In the book *My Glimpse of Eternity,* her astounding, miraculous story is unfolded.

All three of these people are still living and ministering nationwide, in person and through the various media. Their stories can all be fully documented.

No Need for Counterfeits

Stories like these are not a "dime a dozen," but they are frequent and many can be fully verified. But if *all* the professed miracles in modern healing services were genuine, would high-pressure Madison Avenue publicity techniques be necessary for promotion? If all, or even a fraction, of the claims were authentic, no auditorium would be large enough to accomodate the seekers. Jesus was compelled to work in isolated desert areas and even then He was overwhelmed by the crowds. Some prominent in the healing movement have recognized the importance of proper verification. Failure to recognize the necessity of proper documentation, and careless and exaggerated reports of conversions and miracles, may be grieving the Spirit and delaying the greater outpouring the world is waiting for. Although the need may not be the same, many believe that all the power needed to work a miracle is as available today as it was in the days of the Bible. But real faith neither asks nor needs support from the counterfeit.

This is not written by one who is unsympathetic with the Charismatic movement. Following World War I, I was healed from tuberculosis in the last stages. My disability was considered service connected and I spent more than three years in Veterans Bureau hospitals and "out-patient relief" under Veterans Bureau supervision. Then I was miraculously restored in the seclusion of my sleeping porch. For more than fifty-four years I have experienced divine life and now at the age of eighty-four am active in a demanding ministry. This is, therefore, no effort to discredit the supernatural.

I am personally convinced that every believer's life should be a demonstration of the supernatural. I deplore all that smacks of counterfeit, but I wonder if counterfeit is any worse in God's sight than the bald skepticism and unbelief which binds and limits God, and which is so prevalent in many ecclesiastical persuasions. I deplore the activity of much that is branded as "flesh" in the Charismatic movement. But I wonder if the brazen doubt and disbelief, the deadly bondage and stilted worship of many non- and anti-Charismatics, is not as truly of the "flesh." May it not require an enormous amount of phony and exaggerated claims to balance the infidelity and skepticism of the ecclesiastical establishment?

The question is: Why are we so much more afraid of the flesh of emotionalism than we are of the flesh of formalism, skepticism, and unbelief? Is moribund traditionalism and fossilized worship any less of the flesh than exaggerated claims and hyperemotionalism? If we are honestly seeking to avoid "flesh," shouldn't *all* symptoms of the flesh be equally anathema?

A New Call to Holiness

Other objections of non-Pentecostals include the charge of ethical looseness in standards of conduct, particularly in matters of marriage, divorce, and remarriage. Some see a tendency by some Pentecostals to accept and follow a Hollywood lifestyle. Although one Pentecostal leader is quoted as saying that the baptism of the Spirit is exclusively for power, and has nothing to do with the holiness of life, others prominent in the movement disagree.

In the 1978 January-February issue of the *Logos Journal,* Jamie Buckingham acknowledges the need for a more disciplined life-style among Charismatics. On page 9 of this periodical he says, "I anticipate a new call to holiness. Too many charges leveled at Charismatics about their loose way of living are true. Godly leaders will be calling the entire movement to purity. One cannot be filled with the Spirit without wanting to clean up his personal life."

I would like to add my conviction that one cannot be truly born again without wanting to do this. I cannot speak for Jamie Buckingham but I believe he would also agree with this.

A Call by a College President

Other concerned Pentecostal leaders have expressed similar views. One of these is Dr. O. Talmadge Spence, president of Heritage Bible College in Dunn, North Carolina. Dr. Spence has a Pentecostal background and serves a Pentecostal institution.

In an article appearing in the September-October 1973 issue of the magazine *Faith for the Family,* published by Bob Jones University, Dr. Spence says:

There was a time when practical holy living, not tongues, was the final test of Pentecostal religion. The trend now is to tone down the separated life of holiness and emphasize the matter of Holy Ghost manifestations and tongues speaking. Historically

Pentecostalism was born in a Wesleyan or holiness context. Today, the ecstatic utterance of tongues speaking is becoming the mark of the Pentecostalist.

The Wesleyan background is definitely fading from the Pentecostal scene. The doctrine of sanctification is being disassociated from the concept of Pentecostalism. Here again, the same approach to biblical sanctification would have helped to maintain the Pentecostal position. There is a growing clash between power and purity. Pentecost and tongues are often used as tools to gain a kind of power in Pentecostalism that is becoming dangerous to its people.

A consecrated, Christian life, separated from the materialistic worldliness of our time, would have strengthened this people in the battle against the promiscuity and looseness of our day. But what happened to many Methodists years ago is presently developing in Pentecostalism. The former standards of dress, the theater, and divorce are giving way to a general worldliness in Pentecostalism. Suddenly the strong convictions of yesterday are being swept away by these tangents, so extreme they often shock the biblical soul. It seems that many now exploit the gospel to gain the materialistic pleasures they crave.

The biblical, separated life is being classified as archaic and legalistic, with the view that Pentecostalism has now come of age. Although the modern Pentecostal greatly emphasizes evangelism, it is often a shallow evangelism which cannot replace the strong, soul-winning beliefs of yesterday, born of extended prayer and consistent testimony. Great emphasis has been placed upon "the sweet Holy Spirit" and "love" without the realization that we are in a desperate kind of conflict and apostasy. The Pentecostal message is deteriorating into a happy belief that we are in the kingdom age, rather than approaching the Great Tribulation period.

To many, the above appraisal by Dr. Spence seems to be justified. Most denominations, including the Holiness communions, have suffered a general deterioration in standards of holy living. One would expect stronger convictions on standards of separation from the world in externals, amusements, and other worldly practices among those who major in the work of the Holy Spirit. Since He is a *Holy* Spirit, one would expect to find a higher degree of purity and a stricter separation from the world emphasized in the Charismatic renewal. It has been said that if you want to see a worldly appearing group of believers, attend a Charismatic conference or convention. Any protest of this situation is immediately branded as insufferable legalism.

Divorce and Remarriage

Some Charismatics, and some sympathetic non-Charismatics, are concerned about the apparent loss of conviction concerning divorce and remarriage among ecclesiastical and spiritual leaders. To some it seems enigmatic, not to mention the possible violation of biblical principles, that such leaders are frequently divorced and remarried—sometimes more than once. What has happened that multiple-married people are widely featured as conference speakers, spiritual leaders, and radio or television personalities? Although it seems that some of these have fruitful ministries, is there not something wrong with a system which so freely tolerates this practice?

A Respected Leader Speaks

Another of the most highly respected Charismatic leaders has joined Jamie Buckingham and Dr. Spence in the new call to holiness for Charismatics. In an article entitled "Sipping Saints," David Wilkerson says:

> The permissive attitude toward social drinking is fast creeping into the most conservative evangelical church circles. I have spoken at Charismatic conventions where thousands of "Spirit-filled" saints of God lifted their hands in praise and adoration to God—and after being dismissed, numbers of them walked out into the parking lot, opened their trunks and pulled out a couple of six-packs and passed them around to fellow worshippers. Others ordered mixed drinks with their restaurant meals in between the sessions. They returned to speak with "pickled tongues"....
>
> I refuse to give in to the mounting pressures of worldliness—in the disguise of spiritual freedom. What has happened to us, saints of God—when we can sit idly by and not rebuke the fast-eroding morals in the house of God. I believe in free grace, but not licentiousness. I believe in the imputed righteousness of Christ by faith. But I also believe the holiness of God demands that we "touch not that which is unclean."

The Thunder of His Power

In his recent book *The Thunder of His Power*,[4] George Otis, well-known Charismatic teacher and author, has sounded a refreshing and challenging call for a reexamination of life styles by Charismatics. In this book he has sounded a trumpet call for rededication to purity and holiness of life and practice by the members of the renewal.

In the foreword, Campbell McAlpine writes, "Openly and fearlessly George Otis expresses his feelings on the current spiritual climate: The fear of missing *content* [emphasis mine] in renewal, the fear of people being sign followers, tape addicts, and chronic conventioneers. The fear of lack of depth, lack of fear of God and the dangers of little foxes which spoil the vine. The author's intensity of desire for revival proclaims one of revival's greatest needs—holiness.

"Holiness which is God's standard of living, 'Be ye holy, for I am holy,' 'holiness without which no man shall see God,' holiness which is the very nature and character of God and should be the mark of all who claim to be His children through faith in Christ, holiness which is to hate evil and love righteousness, holiness which is the highway to revival." (page 9).

On page 14 George Otis continues the theme: "No subject is more frequently mentioned in the Bible than the holiness of God and His continuous call for a pure, righteous, and holy family. May God forgive us for our failure to give this exciting theme the same priority given by our Lord. No wonder our roots run so shallow."

And from page 67: "Let's face it. Many have drifted

into an appetite for the spectacular. There has been concern for this growing phenomenon over recent years. It has become apparent at the big conferences where the crowds would surge to sessions which high-lighted miracles, leg-lengthening, being slain in the Spirit, super-faith and prosperity teaching. The sessions offering teaching on discipline, growth from crisis, and holy living were sparsely attended."

On page 89 Otis, with wholesome candor, transparency and courage, makes a significant confession of an attitude that has been widespead throughout the renewal. "It is embarrassing to admit how long I was personally a member of that chorus of believers who scoffed at 'those old holiness people.' We joked about their overemphasis on externals: dress, jewelry, movies, alcohol, hair-styles, dancing. 'How misguided,' we said. 'Such kill-joys. Don't they know about our liberties in Christ?'

"We had a point.

"So did they! With the benefit of hindsight it is apparent that many of those holiness preachers were visionaries. In the Spirit, they had seen the latent perils in our generation arising from moral compromises. Their concerns have since proved valid."

In my opinion, in this dynamic, challenging, and stimulating book, George Otis has rendered an important and valuable service to both Charismatics and non-Charismatics. I heartily recommend it to every evangelical Christian.

Conflict Between Power and Purity

Some serious, unbiased observers believe that Charismatics are underemphasizing the *fruits* of the Spirit but overemphasizing, and sometimes even faking, the *gifts* of the Spirit. On the other hand, Charismatics frequently call attention to the soft-pedaling or the total ignoring of the gifts of the Spirit among many other denominations. It is true, as Dr. Spence has suggested, that between the two persuasions there seems to be a conflict between power and purity. Pentecostals stress the power of the filling with the Spirit, including the manifestations of physical healings and other spectacular gifts such as miracles, prophecy, the word of knowledge, etc. Among Holiness groups, purity and cleansing are the paramount emphases, while the gifts are practically ignored. Misunderstanding and antagonism appears to prevail on both sides.

Satanic Glee

If Satan ever feels joy, it must be over the way believers take his bait for controversy, broken fellowships, divisions and disunity in nonessentials. He may not be able to experience joy, but he certainly is gleeful over the small issues that divide and fragment the Church. While no nonessential within itself needs to be divisive, practically all divisions in the true Church have arisen from doctrines that are not essential to salvation. *This means that all broken fellowships within the authentic Church have to be Satan-inspired. Therefore the issue is not who in the Body is right or wrong. The real issue is love, agape love.* Is it possible to be right theoretically and theologically while at the same time being wrong in spirit? The important question again is posed: Which is more important, to be right in opinion or right in spirit? When one is wrong in spirit, the Holy Spirit reacts by an inner witness of grief. This means that He is saying *love, a right spirit, is more important to Him than absolutely correct views.* He may, and therefore does, bless those with opposite views on nonessentials. But He never blesses lovelessness.

Escalating Controversial Viewpoints

Again it is emphasized: There is only *one* answer to division over nonessentials and that is *growth in love, agape love. It will never come any other way.* Since we are fallen beings, the unity of the faith as doctrinal agreement will never come. If the answer to Jesus' prayer for unity in John 17 is ever realized this side of heaven, it will have to come on the basis of unity of the Spirit. This means that we will deliberately cease permitting opinions on nonessentials to produce broken fellowships. *If God will not break fellowship with us over opinions on nonessentials, why should we break fellowship with one another?* Do we not see that the escalation of controversial viewpoints to the point of broken fellowships is satanic?

Love's Resources Sufficient

God knows that fallen minds can never come to perfect agreement and unity on an intellectual, conceptual and doctrinal basis. He knows that many intellectual controversies will never be settled this side of eternity. If Christ's prayer for unity is ever answered on earth, it must be by a different method, and that method is increased love. *"Love never fails"* (1 Cor. 13:8). This means that love's resources are always sufficient.

If that prayer is ever answered in time it will be

through increased love, not by theological agreement. In light of the heart cry of the Savior for the unity of the Body in John 17, *how shall the soul within us longer live if we persist in maintaining division over nonessentials?*

Perhaps you are wondering how we are to reach the required maturity in love. I know of no other way except by a deeper work of the cross, a deeper death to all the life of nature and self. When we are truly willing, God will order the exact set of circumstances that will slay the flesh and increase growth in agape love. Love grows mostly by exercise. For example, accepting differences of opinion without breaking fellowship is one way to produce this growth.

Facing Facts

If this is true—if unity will never come any other way except by an increase of agape love—should we not face and act upon this fact now? *Who knows what a world-shaking revival would follow a demonstration of love that would melt Pentecostals and non-Pentecostals into blessed and holy unity in the Spirit?* If we continue adamantly in our fragmentation, if we continue to defy Christ's plea for unity, who knows what judgment may fall on recreant spiritual leaders and administrators and a divided Church? *Is it possible that the only thing that will unite the Body of Christ is persecution such as exists in Communist lands?* It is said that persecution has wiped out much disunity in the Church where Communism rules. *Is it possible that this is the only way that the Church in the Free World will attain the oneness for which Christ prayed?* If

Christ never offers a prayer that cannot be answered, and if we will not unite any other way, we must prepare for persecution. If love will not unite us, we are inviting judgment.

Not the End of Denominationalism

This does not mean that denominationalism will cease. It means only that *agape love will rise like a mighty flood until all such barriers and walls of partition are inundated and cease to divide.* Agape love is the love that has its origin in God. It is born out of love for God. That love must exceed my love for my own opinion and judgment. Anything less is not agape love, it is self-worship. This quality of love will not only wipe out denominational antagonisms and hostilities, it also will eliminate crippling internecine divisions over personalities and policies within the denominations themselves.

In addition, it will totally solve the problem of factions, parties, and cliques within the local church body. *With this kind of unity, nothing could prevent a worldwide sweep of the kingdom, ushering in the Lord's return.*

"If my people, which are called by my name, shall humble themselves, and pray, and seek my face, *and turn from their wicked ways,* then will I hear from heaven, and will forgive their sin, and will heal their land" (2 Chron. 7:14). This disunity is one of the "wicked ways" from which we must repent to avoid judgment.

The Danger of Exclusive Emphasis

Some qualified observers admit that there is a distinct difference in emphasis between the Holiness and Charismatic movements. They agree that it does seem that one stresses purity while the other stresses power. As Dr. Spence has said, there seems to be a conflict between the two schools on the basic concept of spiritual life. To some analysts it appears that, according to the Scripture, *both emphases are equally important.* It is not possible to overemphasize purity but it seems possible to emphasize it *too exclusively.* It is not possible to overemphasize power but it seems possible also to emphasize it *too exclusively.* It may be that each side is equally guilty of imbalance and needs to learn from the other.

The Holiness movement may have stressed purity too exclusively and the Charismatic stressed power too exclusively. Until more recently, the Holiness movement has taught a rather strict standard of separation from the world as represented by Hollywood. It has made much of purity of heart and life, freedom from pride, evil temper, and other carnal manifestations of the flesh. But its teachers have largely ignored teaching on the gifts of the Spirit. They have claimed that purity *is* power, but they have confined the operation of that power mostly to the realm of the Spirit as demonstrated in holy living both inwardly and outwardly. They have emphasized ethics as a test of the Spirit-filled life. This has subjected them to the charge of legalism by many Charismatics. On the other hand, the dynamic that characterized the early days of the Holiness movement seems largely to have dissipated.

Ignoring the Gifts

While insisting on a high standard of ethics and the power to live a holy, separated life, most of the Holiness teachers and theologians have ignored the gifts of the Spirit such as healing, prophecy, the word of knowledge and wisdom, faith and the working of miracles. They acknowledge the operation of all gifts in the early Church. Although they do not claim that the gifts ceased with the Apostolic age, as Reformed theology does, they have so largely neglected them that their silence is almost tantamount to the Reformed position.

All of them would unequivocally declare that "Jesus Christ is the same yesterday, today and forever." But many of them strictly hedge their stand. This difference is basic. It is a watershed. Not many of them would agree that if God had His way all the gifts of the Spirit would be present and operating in the Church today in a similar proportion as in the early Church. Among many there is an inordinate fear of fanaticism and a greater fear of counterfeit than of grieving God through unbelief. It is unclear which attitude is the greater tragedy. *Unbelief ties the hands of God as truly as falseness, sham, and exaggeration grieves Him. One is as truly of the flesh as the other.*

At this point I again suggest that the real problem is not who is right and who is wrong; not even who is most nearly right. The problem is *deficient love.* A proper appreciation of the supremacy of *agape love,* that is, love for God Himself, would wipe out all misunderstandings and antagonisms, elevate all parties above shattering controversies, unite the fragmented Body of Christ, and bring her Lord great joy.

7

SEEKING TO HEAL THE BREACH—II

A Third Group

Thus far, our attention has been focused largely on differences between the Holiness movement and the Charismatics. In a letter to the author, Dr. T. W. Hunt, faculty member of Southwestern Baptist Theological Seminary, Fort Worth, Texas, called attention to another group of Evangelicals who share similar reservations, even to the point of prejudice against Charismatics. This group consists of churches known as Fundamentalist Churches, Bible Churches and certain main-line denominations, many of whom hold to the Calvinist or Reformed theology. Although some of these insist on elevating purity of doctrine above fellowship with "outsiders," Dr. Hunt says, "this group also has been influenced by the emphasis on the Holy Spirit." Following is an extract from his letter:

The third group mentioned above has also been influenced by the emphasis on the Holy Spirit. Many Evangelicals in this group believe that there is a deeper life, a filling with the Holy Spirit, but their differences arise in the timing and the method of its bestowal and its appreciation. They believe that contained within the salvation experience itself is all that God wants to give, but the appropriation of various depths and the gifts of the Spirit are ap-

propriated according to the will of the Christian co-
operating with God. That is, they are saying that
what is called by Charismatics and Holiness groups
a "second work of grace" is actually a "renewal" or
"filling" which was contained in and even implicit in
the original regeneration experience, although not
fully grasped at the time of salvation. Thus, salvation is, in their eyes, a comprehensive program of
regeneration, filling and holiness of life. Usually not
all is understood or grasped at salvation, but may
be appropriated as the Christian grows.

Appropriation and exercise of spiritual gifts is, to
some extent, voluntary, whereas bestowal was
implicit in the salvation experience. Thus, salvation
or new birth is itself the "baptism in the Holy
Spirit," but the appropriation of spiritual privileges
is sometimes subsequent to the experience of the
"baptism" [i.e. initial salvation].

This group often refers to "being filled with the
Spirit" as an experience subsequent to salvation
and, like Charismatics, they contrast "carnal Christians" with "Spirit-filled Christians." They would
share with Charismatics a belief that God has for
them a depth of life, spiritual gifts, plus supernatural
and miraculous intervention. They might share with
their Holiness brethren a conviction that this deep-
ening experience leads to new levels of holiness of
life and separation. Yet they differ from both, main-
ly in the terminology concerning time of bestowal
and appropriation. Following such a renewal, they
normally move into a new period of praise, joy, fellowship—exactly as Charismatics—and, on occas-

ion, some even speak in tongues, but usually insist that their first encounter with Christ sufficed to supply them with the gift....

It is clear that the emphasis on the Holy Spirit has influenced the third group mentioned above very greatly. Many of the great Christian publishing houses are issuing books on the work of the Holy Spirit, being filled with the Spirit (rather than "baptized with the Spirit"); Bible colleges sponsor seminars on the work of the Spirit; sermons are preached on the subject, and many seek eagerly the "filling with the Spirit" or the "Spirit-filled life," or the "Spirit-filled walk"....

Even the Fundamentalist and main-line denominations sometimes acknowledge an indebtedness to the Charismatic movement, if not in words, at least in direction. Never before has the work of the Holy Spirit been so emphasized and His role in changing, equipping, guiding and perfecting life been so appreciated as in the last several years. It seems quite likely that these new directions have to some degree been affected by the emphasis originally generated by the Charismatic movement.

Observations by a "Third Group" Pastor

Typical of the disagreements between this third group and Charismatics (though they share large areas of mutual understanding and sympathy) are those expounded and elucidated in a recent book entitled *The Charismatics,* authored by John F. MacArthur, Jr. and published by Zondervan Publishing House. Dr. MacArthur is pastor of Grace Community Church of the Valley, Panorama City, California.

MacArthur is a non-Charismatic who, in my opinion, has something important to say to Charismatics. I believe the Charismatic movement could profit by giving him a sympathetic ear. In fact, by his "objective," penetrating, and discriminating analysis of the Charismatic movement, he may have rendered an invaluable service to both the Charismatics and non-Charismatics within the Body of Christ. His book may be considered by some as a negative critique, but Charismatics who are not opportunistic or wedded to a theology which they feel compelled to defend and maintain by reason of personal or vested interests will welcome some of his criticisms. They will devoutly pray that these might help produce a more balanced perspective and a more viable credibility. Those who love the movement most will be the first to acknowledge the importance of being sensitive to honest critics of the movement. Although not everyone may be sufficiently delivered from spiritual egoism to lend an ear, many mature spiritual leaders, including respected educators and intellectuals, consider honest critics as their best friends. One derogates, calumniates, or ignores them at his own peril. Hopefully, Charismatic leaders are sufficiently humble and broken to give attention to a capable and competent student of the movement.

Extracts from MacArthur's book appeared in the October, November, and December 1979 issues of *Moody Monthly*. It is from this condensation that quotes are taken and upon which the following observations are based.

Dr. MacArthur raises some questions which must have occured to many who are sympathetic to the re-

newal. One of these is the question of continuing revelation. He charges that Charismatics hold "that the
Bible is not our final source of God's revelation" but
simply a "witness" to additional revelation that He is
giving today; that Christians can add to the Bible, and
that they can accept such additions as normative, and
that the Bible is only a "model" for what the Holy
Spirit is doing today to inspire believers.

"Charismatics believe that God sends new revela-
tions on a continuing basis. They are making myriad
claims that God speaks to them through tongues,
prophecies, and visions."

After this damaging charge, MacArthur adds,
"Although Charismatics will deny that they are trying
to add to Scripture, their views on prophetic utterance,
gifts of prophecy, and revelation do just that" (*Moody
Monthly,* October 1979, pages 20-21).

If true, this is terrifying to me. While I believe that
only the lunatic fringe of Charismatics would be guilty
of this charge, I suggest that MacArthur has laid a
finger upon a possible danger spot. This should call
Charismatics to a clear-cut and unequivocal stand on
this question. MacArthur's warning upon this crucial
and important perspective should not be ignored. In
my opinion, when he says, "Christians must not loosely
interpret the meaning of inspiration and revelation..."
and when he says, "It has always been important to be
able to separate God's Word from that which is false"
and "If we then undermine the uniqueness of the Bible,
we will have no way of distinguishing God's voice from
man's voice," he sounds an important caution which all
but the most irresponsible will heed.

Those who most love and appreciate what God is doing through the Charismatics will see the possibility of the existence of a revelational "gray" area here and will religiously seek to avoid it.

Dr. MacArthur puts his finger upon another soft place in the Charismatic theology. He suggests that Charismatics have a tendency to exalt experience above Scripture (*Moody Monthly,* November 1979, page 38). Most Charismatics would emphatically deny this but there seems to be some basis for it. As an illustration, he cites the testimony of one woman who reports that she was given a new "belly button." Another testifies that she has taught her dog to praise the Lord in an unknown bark, and others claim that water has been changed into gasoline in an automobile tank much as Jesus changed water into wine.

Dr. MacArthur admits these are bizarre examples but insists they are not rare. He further claims that one well-known Charismatic writer, Larry Christenson, in his book *Speaking in Tongues* (Dimension Books), has often indicated that the Christian faith is based on experience and that theology is only an explanation of that experience (*Moody Monthly,* November 1979, page 40). I read this book but did not gain this impression.

I admit that these illustrations seem rather ridiculous and damaging to the witness of Charismatics; but they do seem to represent a frame of mind not wholly unknown among them. If the story of water turning into wine were not in the Bible, very few would believe it no matter what its source. All of us know that nothing is impossible with God. We understand that many of His acts are superrational—but they are not usually absurd or irrational. Most Charismatics would agree with Dr. MacArthur that "all experience must be validated by the more sure word of Scripture. When we seek the truth about Christian life and doctrine, we don't go to someone's experience. We go to the revealed Word of God" (*Moody Monthly,* November 1979, page 38). I believe that the leaders and theologians of the Charismatic movement could profit by acknowledging possible weaknesses and giving better guidance. It is doubtful if extreme sensationalism strengthens credibility. Dr. MacArthur pinpoints several other possible vulnerable positions and practices of the Charismatic culture.

However, his book also challenges the basic theology of the Charismatics. He apparently accepts the Reformed position that there is no such an experience as "a second work of grace, subsequent to regeneration" (*Moody Monthly,* December 1979, pages 82, 83). In addition, he takes positive exception to the interpretation of Hebrews 13:8 that the first century Church is God's ideal for the entire Church age: that if God had His way, all the gifts of the Spirit would be present and manifest in the Church today in a similar proportion as in the early Church. Apparently he believes that the age of miracles is past, that it ended with the Apostolic age as did all the sign-gifts of the Spirit (*Moody Monthly,* December 1979, pages 83,84). On page 20 of the October issue of the same magazine, he sounds a warning with which some responsible Charismatics would agree. There he says, "Today's Charismatics run a course perilously close to the Church at Corinth, where spiritual gifts were counterfeited." On page 44 of the November issue he charges that a lot of counterfeit gifts are passing for the real today, and that accepting the counterfeit forfeits the genuine. According to Billy Graham and other sympathetic critics of the movement, this is one thing which greatly weakens Charismatic credibility. All true friends of the movement lament any basis for this indictment and charge.

In his discussion of hermeneutics and the principles to guide sound biblical interpretation, as far as those of his own theological persuasion are concerned, Dr. MacArthur practically demolishes the theology of the Charismatics. He questions or outright rejects as unbiblical most of their basic theological distinctives.

Yet his book *The Charismatics* presents what seems to some a strange but wholesome anomaly: The Charismatic theological tree is bad, but in spite of this, according to his book, it bears remarkably good fruit. On page 82 of the December issue of *Moody Monthly,* his appraisal of the movement is astonishingly positive, appreciative, almost ecstatic. Listen. "We can thank God for Charismatic and Pentecostal people." His reason is that "they believe the Bible and hold it up as authoritative." He praises God that "they believe in the deity of Jesus Christ, His sacrificial death, His physical resurrection, salvation by faith not works, the need to live in obedience to Christ and proclaim the faith with zeal" (*Moody Monthly,* December 1979, page 82). If the tree is known by its fruit, this doesn't seem too bad.

I have seldom read a more complimentary evaluation of the movement's worth than in portions of this stimulating work. With remarkable candor he says,

"The Charismatic movement has made an impact on the Church possibly unparalleled in history" (*Moody Monthly,* October 1979, page 19). Beginning on page 48 of the November 1979 issue, he sounds like a dedicated Charismatic apologist: "Non-Charismatics have a tremendously important lesson to learn from Charismatics who have stepped into the void in many a dead church situation to give people a meaningful spiritual experience." Among their many other virtues he cites the following: "While they place great emphasis on ecstatic experiences and miracles of all kinds, Charismatics do study God's Word....In Charismatic churches, one almost always finds a strong leader.... Charismatics are known for their warmth, love, excitement, and enthusiasm....The Church was never meant to be a mental mausoleum....Human effort will never replace the work of the Spirit. One favor the Charismatics have done the Church is to help us recognize that the Church needs more than seminary graduates, beautifully written Sunday School curricula, and an organizational chart that would rival General Motors.

"Charismatics have helped pull the Church up short to realize that God's Spirit will build the Church, not human ingenuity.... It is impressive to see what the Charismatics have managed to do by way of getting their people involved in Bible studies, seminars, conferences, business men's groups, etc." A dedicated Charismatic could hardly have done better.

On page 19 of the October number of this magazine, an important question is raised: "I've asked myself, 'Are all those people who are supposedly having all those amazing experiences really right after all?' " But in my opinion, this is not the basic question. The real question in the controversy between Charismatics and non-Charismatics is not who is right or who is wrong in these nonessential matters. The question is not even who is most nearly right. The real question which concerns heaven is: Are we sufficiently mature in *agape love?* Do we love God enough to love, accept and fellowship with those whom God loves, accepts and fellowships with—regardless of opinions in things nonessential to salvation? It is not primarily a question of horizontal love—love for one another. It is a question of love for God Himself. "Everyone that loveth him that begot loveth him also that is begotten of him" (1 John 5:1).

On page 83 of the December issue of *Moody Monthly,* Dr. MacArthur says: "To be baptized by the Holy Spirit [that is, in initial salvation] means that Christ places us, by means of the Spirit, into the unity of His Body and gives us a common life principle that connects us with everyone else who also believes in Christ. Baptism with the Spirit [that is, initial salvation] makes all believers one." I submit that if this is true, there should be no schism in the Body because fellowship should be on the basis of a common life and relationship rather than a common opinion on nonessentials. Nothing should permit rejection of another member of the same family except his broken relationship with the Father.

I suggest that in these profound and meaningful pronouncements Dr. MacArthur has abolished all occasion for fragmentation in the Body of Christ.

Observations by a "Third Group" Theologian

A prominent scholar and theologian from this designated "Third Group" associated with a main-line school of theology is Dr. J. I. Packer. The March 7, 1980 issue of *Christianity Today* carried a significant essay on the Charismatic renewal by this noted English theologian and Professor of Systematic and Historial Theology at Regent College, Vancouver, British Columbia. While his treatment of this subject is in general agreement with Dr. MacArthur in his book *The Charismatics,* Dr. Packer, suggests the possibility of significant rapport between Charismatics and non-Charismatics of all theological persuasions, including the Fundamentalists and the Reformed.

In his approach to this subject, Dr. Packer fully recognizes the questions and issues that divide the two camps. He neither minimizes nor ignores them. He is aware of the weaknesses, liabilities, and criticisms observed and voiced by non-Charismatics such as: "...the elevation of experience above truth or doctrine, the irrationality of glossalalia, spiritual pride and arrogance [which he calls "elitism" because it implies that non-Charismatics are substandard Christians], and its alleged disruptiveness, resulting in church splits." He "doubts" Charismatic restorationism, suggesting that Pentecost was "a singular, unrepeatable moment." "Nor is there any way to make good the claim that the sign-gifts that authenticated the Apostles...are now restored."

But these problems do not seem greatly to bother him. With rare and admirable humility of spirit he has accepted the Charismatic brethren into full fellowship in the Spirit, notwithstanding doctrinal differences. With refreshing deliverance from theological and doctrinal elitism and snobbery, with commendable appreciation and deference to those with whom he disagrees, he declares: "Yet one can doubt restorationism [a restoring of first century experience] and still rejoice in the real enrichment that Charismatics have found in seeking the Lord. Their call to expectant faith in the God who still, on occasion, heals supernaturally and does wonders can be gratefully heard, and their challenge to seek radical personal renewal can be humbly received without accepting their theology. *We should be glad that our God does not hide His face from those who seek Him—neither from Charismatics nor non-Charismatics—until their theology is correct. Where would any of us be if He did? And we should not refuse to learn from Charismatics while contesting some of their opinions*" (emphasis mine).

Here is a theologian of the first rank from this "Third Group," a scholar from the Anglican school of theology, who is suggesting that Charismatics and non-Charismatics may fellowship on the basis of a common life and relationship rather than a common opinion on nonessentials. Quote: "Despite some unhappy theology, the Charismatic movement overall bears marks of genuine spiritual renewal, and though it or sections of it may have lessons to learn in doctrine, it has its own lessons to teach concerning practice." In other words, he is saying that the street between them is a two-way street and that each can and should learn from the other.

As a non-Charismatic, with becoming humility and

candor, Dr. Packer continues: "Without advocating the practices mentioned [that is, of the Charismatics] or any technique of 'working up' meetings (for manufactured excitement never communicates God), I urge that the Charismatic purpose is right. Charismatic practice, however childish or zany it may seem on the surface, convicts the restrained, formal behavior in church that passes for reverence."

Dr. Packer is a happy illustration of our main thesis that fellowship between born-again believers should be on the basis of a common origin, a common parenthood, a common family relationship rather than a common opinion on nonessentials. The unity for which Christ prayed will never come any other way.

8

THE BRIDGE IS AGAPE LOVE

"Knowledge Puffs Up, but Love Builds Up"
(1 Corinthians 8:1 *NIV*)

I consider this to be the most important chapter in this book. All that has previously been advanced is in preparation for what follows.

The only power that will bring unity in the Body of Christ is the power of agape love. Adequate love for Jesus enables one to accept and love those whom *He* accepts and loves, regardless of their opinions in nonessentials. *We shall never be united by conceptual truth, church polity, liturgy, or any canon or confession of faith—only by agape love.* With a sufficient flow of love in the Body, all divisive factors will shrink and diminish in significance. Increasing love will cover all differences concerning nonessentials to salvation and bring the oneness for which Christ prayed.

The Supreme Priority of Agape Love

No breach in the Body of Christ is caused primarily by superior knowledge, differing convictions, or divergent views of truth; but by one thing and only one— *lack of agape love.* Therefore, the only remedy will be found in growth in love, that is, authentic love for God. Mark this well: In any controversy over nonessentials, the question is not primarily who is right; not even who is most nearly right. The real question is, Is there sufficient maturity in love of God to cover differences of opinion in nonessentials and unite the Body? Is there sufficient deliverance from *idolatry of personal opinion* to enable those of different views to accept and fellowship with those whom God accepts? Can the Church comprehend that all differences in nonessentials provide a means for practicing agape love? Can the Church comprehend that in God's book increase in agape love has *supreme* priority, priority over all other considerations?

Since God Himself is *infinite truth* and certainly knows which view is correct in any controversy, why did He leave room for so many differences of opinion? He knows that finite minds will never reach absolutely inerrant conclusions. He knows that many controversies will never be settled this side of heaven. If infallibility in doctrine or conceptual truth in nonessentials is *all important* in God's sight, why did He leave room for doubts and differences of opinion? May it not be that He permits uncertainty in nonessentials to give opportunity for practice and growth in love? Has the Church ever comprehended the importance to God of love for one another, love for other members of God's own beloved family? Since learning agape love is the supreme goal of life on earth (see *Don't Waste Your Sorrows*), He is more interested in our maturity in love than in settling academic questions. Can this be denied? *In God's book, the important thing is not to settle controversial issues here and now, but while considering them, to grow in grace and in the supreme virtue of agape love.*

Satan's Bait

If this is true, how silly of us to take Satan's bait and become involved in disputes which both God and Satan know will never be settled here, instead of using them to practice and mature in love. How silly to be chasing "red herrings" of controversy instead of majoring on the one goal of supreme importance—growing in agape love.

All theologians, administrators, and other spiritual leaders who persist in fragmentation of the Body of Christ over nonessentials may be risking the loss of eternal rank in a social order where the law of love is supreme. The question is, How are you going to explain at the judgment seat of Christ why you refused to offer fellowship to other born-again members of Christ's Body?

Spiritual Absurdity

Why should anyone break fellowship over a difference of opinion, especially when it concerns only nonessentials? Doesn't this seem senseless, futile, even absurd? In the first place, we are considering an opinion only, that is, "a belief not based on absolute certainty" (*Webster*). And it concerns a nonessential, a belief that is not fundamental to salvation. For instance, a belief in the method or mode of water baptism is not generally considered as fundamental or indispensable to salvation. Some believe that the Bible supports the method of sprinkling, others that it teaches the method of immersion, and still others insist that the Biblical way is immersion three times face forward. Each of these differing beliefs would be considered by most people as opinions only and as not essential to salvation. *Does it not seem strange, even senseless, that anyone should break fellowship because of differences of opinion in such instances?* If the opinion could be considered equivalent to the absolute truth or inspired by the same authority as Scripture (which it is not), only then would a break in fellowship be justified. Remember Romans 14.

Pride of Opinion Equals Spiritual Pride

The question remains, Why should anyone break fellowship over differences of opinion in nonessentials? There is only one answer, and that is *lack of agape love issuing from pride,* not pride of wealth or of fame or achievement, but *pride of opinion*—that is, *spiritual pride.* And spiritual pride is just as carnal as any other. *This may be an understatement.* Many of us would be horrified to realize that we are victims of pride of face, race, social standing, wealth, fame, or personal accomplishments. But multitudes of us have succumbed to spiritual pride, pride of opinion, and that may be more fleshly than other forms because it more often rends the Body of Christ and causes multitudes to be lost. In addition, it brings untold grief to the heart of Christ (John 17). In spite of this, the Church at large and its spiritual leaders seem to remain complacent, comfortable, defensive, even aggressive in justification of opinions in nonessentials that produce fragmentation in the Body. Should we not face up to this fact?

We profess to be saved, sanctified, filled with the Spirit. Yet eminent pastors, famous evangelists, outstanding theologians, leaders and administrators in every ecclesiastical division are guilty of this detestable pride. Reemphasizing, this is a pride that may be more carnal and destructive than other forms which we so vehemently abhor and condemn as sinful, because it is more deadly to the Body of Christ and the salvation of souls. *Someday we may discover that pride of opinion is a greater sin than the supposedly incorrect doctrine over which we have broken fellowship.*

Pride of Opinion—a Form of Idolatry

The real issue between Charismatics and non-Charismatics and their theologians is not a matter of tongues, whether everyone should speak in tongues or whether nobody should. The real issue goes far deeper. In the opinion of many, there is not enough difference in their theology to justify antagonism. Both Charismatic and non-Charismatic schools of Evangelicals believe in all the fundamentals of salvation. Both profess belief in inerrancy of the Word and both claim undying love for Christ. Both teach Hebrews 13:8, "Jesus Christ, the same yesterday, and today, and forever." How can their hostility be explained? The only possible answer is, insufficient love for God. Pride of opinion in nonessentials transcends love; and that is not only sin, it is the worst form of sin—it is idolatry. We set up our opinions as little icons and demand that all others bow down and worship them by agreeing with us. Those who do not, we separate from our fellowship This may be the essence of carnal pride, even idolatry. When we demand that others agree with us in nonessentials on pain of rejection, are we not in danger of reproaching God for failure to correct their error Himself?

But that is not all. Breaking fellowship over a difference of opinion in a nonessential may reveal not only a carnal pride but the deeper reason for that pride, a pathological spiritual ego. Inordinate admiration, esteem, and loyalty to one's opinions and theological concepts in nonessentials is actually self-worship, even though unconscious. To be affronted by nonacceptance of a pet opinion to the point of rejecting a brother indicates a bloated and diseased ego. It is a sort of "love me, love my dog" syndrome.

Opinion and Prestige

To sacrifice one's opinions to the opinions of another requires a humility strange to most of us. Our opinions seem to be among our most priceless possessions. Our prestige is so closely associated with our opinions that the successful promotion of our opinions is tantamount to the promotion of our ego.

This may be an exaggeration, but it sometimes appears that for some of us it is more difficult and requires more agape love to surrender opinions, even on nonessentials, than to give up wealth, health, fame, position, reputation, even life itself. It seems that some of us would almost prefer physical to idealistic martyrdom.

Broken Fellowships—Satan Inspired

Because no nonessential intrinsically compels division, practically all divisions in the *authentic Church* have occured over doctrines, policy or polity that are nonessential to salvation. *Think of it!* This means that all broken fellowships in the true Church are wholly and entirely Satan inspired. None of them are heaven-born or Spirit-initiated. Again, it is insisted that the real issue is not who is right or who is wrong. The real issue is *love, the love that covers.* When one breaks fellowship with a born-again brother over a nonessential, is it not because his love for his opinion outweighs his love for his brother? Does anyone doubt that the fragmentation of the Church, the Body of Christ, could be prevented by sufficient maturity in love? And what about a world with over a billion unevangelized souls awaiting word of Christ's love? Can these millions be reached without a united Body?

Right in Opinion—Wrong in Spirit

Is it possible to be right theoretically and theologically while wrong in spirit, that is, lacking in love? *Which is more important, to be right in opinion and wrong in spirit or to be wrong in opinion and right in spirit?* What happens when one is wrong in spirit? Is not the Holy Spirit within him consciously grieved and does He not witness to offense by an inward sense of disapproval? *God may, and does, bless those with opposite views on nonessentials.* Can this be denied? The Baptists are strong on water baptism. The Friends just as sincerely abstain. God has blessed them both. This means that God is saying, *"There is something more important than absolutely correct views—that is, agape love."* He is saying that a right spirit, which is love, is more important to Him than correct theological opinions. He may and does bless those with contradictory views but He never blesses lovelessness. To be right in opinion and wrong in spirit is virtually to be altogether wrong.

The Only Answer

Allow me to reemphasize, there is only one answer to division over nonessentials and *that is increased love, love for God Himself. It will never come any other way.* While we are fallen beings, the unity of faith, that is, theological agreement, will never come. If the answer to Jesus' prayer for unity in John 17 is ever realized this side of heaven, it will have to be in the realm of the Spirit. This means that we will cease to permit opinions in nonessentials to produce schism in the Body. If God does not break fellowship with us over opinions, some of which He knows are erroneous, *why should we break fellowship with one another?* Does this not indicate that the escalation of controversial views to the point of schism is Satanic? Please read again the poem by Charles Wesley in Chapter 3.

A Basic Question

This important question demands attention. If all born-again people are members of the same Body, should not all born-again people fellowship with one another regardless of positions on nonessentials? This is a basic question. *Everything hangs on the answer to this.* If this is accepted, the problem of division is solved. It is as simple as that. If anyone claims this is impossible, he is suggesting that Jesus prayed a prayer that cannot be answered. If anyone has a viable alternative, I welcome it.

Although we may not coerce the thinking of others, we may fellowship with them regardless. If they refuse fellowship, they bear their own responsibility.

> "He drew a circle that shut me out,
>   Heretic, rebel, a thing to flout;

But Love and I had the wit to win—
We drew a circle and took him in."
—Edwin Markham

We Be Brethren

If you are scripturally born again you are a member of the Body of Christ and a son of my very own Father. As a member of the same family, you are my own brother, whether you realize it or acknowledge it or not. As far as I am concerned, this is true whether you are a Charismatic or anti-Charismatic; whether you believe that everyone should speak in tongues or whether you believe that speaking in tongues is of the devil; whether you believe that the gifts of the Spirit are in operation in the Church today or whether you believe they ceased at the close of the Apostolic age; whether you are a Calvinist and believe in the "Five Points" or whether you are an Arminian and believe that the "Five Points" are heresy; whether you believe in eternal security or in falling from grace; whether you accept only the "King James" or prefer a modern version; whether you believe in baptismal regeneration or no ordinances at all; whether you believe in immersion or sprinkling, infant or adult baptism; whether you wash feet or don't; whether you are a Methodist, Baptist, Presbyterian, Disciples of Christ, Church of Christ, Mennonite, Amish, Seventh Day Adventist, Episcopalian, Catholic...or no denomination at all; whether you believe in female or only male ordination; whether you think that Saturday is the true Sabbath and should be kept holy or whether you think that the day is indifferent; whether you eat meat or are a vegetarian; whether you drink coffee, tea and soft drinks or only water, fruit juices and milk; whether you wear a toupee or sport a bald head; whether you color your hair or not; whether you are a pre-, a post-, or an amillennialist; whether you are a Republican, a Democrat or a Socialist; whether your skin is white, black, red, brown or yellow; and if there be any other doubtful matters or silly nonessentials over which we differ...if you are born again, we still are members of the same family and organic parts of the same spiritual Body. I may think some of your beliefs are as crazy as a loon, but if I have sufficient love for God, agape love, I will not reject you as a person.

All Fragmentation Satan-inspired

All fragmentation of the Body of Christ is Satan-inspired. He is out to divide and conquer. Why have we been too stupid to recognize this? Fragmentation is not the result of superior wisdom, greater intelligence or superlative judgment, deeper piety or more supreme devotion and dedication to God and eternal truth. It is always from the devil, who often is transformed into an angel of light (2 Cor. 11:14). One may have his own opinions on all of these points—as I have. I haven't relinquished or modified my former basic views on any important point. I believe I have grown, however, in agape love, that is, love for God Himself, and in my conviction that God is God and that all of us should cease attempting to "play God" to others. "They are God's servants, not yours. They are responsible to Him, not to you. Let Him tell them whether they are right or wrong. And God is able to make them do as they should" (Rom. 14:4 *LB*).

When one refuses to fellowship with another who is organically united to the Body of Christ because he differs on nonessential matters, he is not only creating schism in the Body but bringing grief to the heart of Christ. He has been "conned" by the one who masquerades as an angel of light. To unnecessarily break fellowship with a member of the Body is similar to cutting off a finger, an arm or a leg from his own body. If we believe there is a Church Universal, can we deny this? Why don't respected theologians and spiritual leaders on both sides of these controversies understand this and lead the way to repentance, rapprochement and reconciliation?

Greed

In addition to pride of opinion, mentioned previously, there is another relevant consideration...and that is financial. Is it possible that fear of monetary loss motivates us in the maintenance of sectarian barriers? Although some of us teach that God alone is the source of all wealth and material resources, do we continue to foster division in the fear that others may tap our financial reservoir? Only a living faith and boundless agape love can deliver one from inordinate greed and heal this breach. The principal reason for intense denominational, sectarian competition and antagonism often is not zeal for truth but pure, plain, unvarnished selfishness and greed. And this is sin (Eph. 5:5). Those guilty of this sin may succeed in building an earthly kingdom, but it will perish in the blazing conflagration of the judgment. No correct doctrine, beautiful liturgy, or proper church government can cure this.

Only a mighty baptism of genuine love for God Himself. Correct doctrine, correct views are important—but these are *not all important.* There is something more supremely important and that is *agape love.* Can the Church, its leaders, theologians, educators and administrators comprehend that in God's book *agape love is the supreme virtue, the supreme wisdom, the supreme power,* the heart of the essence of holiness and Godlikeness?

The Faith of God

What is the faith of God? I am convinced it is God's infinite confidence that agape love is supreme—the ultimate power in the universe. Why and how was this question raised? At some point following the original creation, Lucifer lost this faith and rebelled, thereby challenging the faith of God. At that moment Satan, the fallen Lucifer, embraced the belief that pride, deception, subterfuge, coercion...the might and power of hatred, malevolence and brute force...all that constitutes what is known as the flesh, such as sexual impurity, vice, discord, self-centeredness, self-indulgence, and self-adulation (issuing in an overwhelming ambition and determination to be supreme in the universe)—all of these, he decided, were a force more potent than agape love.

Ultimate Reality

Hebrews 12:1 indicates that there is an invisible world which possesses as viable a reality (or even a more viable reality) as the visible world in which we live. In this passage the writer to the Hebrews envisions the heroes of faith of the preceding chapter as spectators of scenes on earth, and as surrounding those who are running the heavenly race. "Therefore, since we are surrounded by such a great cloud of witnesses [the heroes of faith],...let us run with perseverance the race marked out for us" (*NIV*). The writer here suggests that inhabitants of the invisible world live on one side of something like a see-through mirror. Our world is visible to them, but because we live on the other side of the mirror, theirs is invisible to us. To this present throbbing moment, the world at large (including the Church) has suffered under the illusion that only the visible, material universe constitutes reality. But if we understand the Word, *ultimate* reality is confined to the realm of the immaterial and invisible. Paul's references in Ephesians and Colossians to angelic hosts, principalities and powers, thrones and dominions, which are invisible, celestial potentates including rulers of the darkness of this world—these give unmistakable evidence of an ordered, organized, and structured hierarchy of spirit intelligences of various elevations in rank, honor and authority. We do not know the extent of this unseen population but it is probably as much greater than the population of earth as the limitless galactic systems of boundless outer space are greater than our planetary system. And this unseen and apparently infinite universe consitutes *ultimate reality* because the inspired writers insist that the present order of things is passing away (1 Cor. 7:31).

A Controlled Experiment

Now here is the "mind blower." In Ephesians 3:10, Paul reveals that God is using the Church to prove to the entire universe—of which the unseen is probably the inconceivably greater part—that agape love is the ultimate and supreme power and authority. Listen. "His intent was that now, *through the Church,* the manifold wisdom of God should be made known to the rulers and authorities in the heavenly realms, according to his eternal purpose which he accomplished in Christ Jesus our Lord" (*NIV,* emphasis mine). Therefore, the eyes of the entire universe are focused upon the Church—not on business, not on governments, not on armies or navies, but on the Church.

Because Satan challenged God's faith that agape love is the supreme power, God is conducting a controlled universe-wide experiment and demonstration in which He is using the Church to verify, exemplify, and prove to the spectators that agape love *is* the ultimate, the supreme authority. This experiment and demonstration began with Satan's fall and will end with his final incarceration in the lake of fire and the glorious enthronement of the Lamb and His Bride. This is why God is so interested in the unity of the Church. Every broken fellowship, every wound in the Body, every fragmented relationship proclaims to a waiting, watching universe that the Church is not yet fully convinced that agape love is supreme. Strife in the Body of Christ, masquerading as love for God and eternal truth, is actually a witness to the entire universe that the Church is still influenced by satanic deception. The only way the Church can make known the manifold wisdom of God is by practicing God's way of agape love in interpersonal, denominational, and interdenominational relationships, keeping God's new commandment of not only to love God but to love one another.

Supreme Evidence of Agape Love—Martyrdom

The supreme evidence of love for God is giving your life for God and one another. The most convincing testimony to the population of the unseen world that agape love is supreme—the most powerful force in the universe—is the vast number of Christian martyrs. Perhaps this is God's reason for permitting martyrdom. "This is how we know what love is: Jesus Christ laid down his life for us. And we ought to lay down our lives for our brothers" (1 John 3:16 *NIV*). In surrendering his life for the very love of God and Christ's Church, every martyr "casts his vote" for God in this controlled experiment. Satan has no martyrs, only victims. To the visible and invisible watching worlds, the millions of martyrs testify to a faith that agape love is supreme. By the same token, a steadfast faith in God under adversity, affliction and persecution, including a sacrificial and abstemious life-style, testifies to the Church's faith that agape love is supreme.

The most convincing proof to the world that agape love is supreme is not that we are always delivered from hardship, affliction, poverty and suffering, but that none of these separate us, not only from *His love* for *us,* but from *our love* for *Him.* This love enables one to say with the hymn writer:

> "Go then worldly fame and pleasure,
>   Come disaster, toil and pain;
>   In thy service, pain is pleasure,
>   In thy labor, loss is gain."

God's Risk

Since God is willing to risk His government for all eternity on this faith, isn't it strange that so few of us are willing to risk our moment-by-moment and day-by-day relationships on it? Lapsing into the flesh of self-defense, judgmentalism, rejection and lovelessness leaves the Body scarred and wounded and destroys its testimony to a watching universe. A life-style of self-indulgence, self-seeking and self-promotion is a vote for Satan's concept. To justify God's faith in using the Church to make known the manifold wisdom of God, she must be totally united. This is why the *love that covers* and heals wounds and unites the Body is more important to God than correctness in the most important nonessential doctrine.

Agape Love—the Ultimate Weapon

All authority over Satan, all authority in the moral and spiritual realm, originates from and is generated by agape love. All deficiency in the moral and spiritual realm is the deficiency of love. Whenever one lapses into the flesh of lovelessness, authority over Satan ceases.

Agape love is the ultimate weapon against Satan. It is energy more powerful than atomic energy. It so powerfully repelled Satan that it expelled him from the heavenly sphere. This is why he is allergic to worship and praise, because it is the supreme expression of agape love—love for God. We may some day discover that it was the volume of worship and praise for the Almighty by Michael and his angels that devastated and cast out Satan and his angels from the celestial sphere. This is not surprising in view of the victory over Israel's enemies by Jehoshaphat's choir of singers and praisers, as related in 2 Chronicles 20.

All spiritual growth is growth primarily in one thing—agape love. All spiritual immaturity is immaturity primarily in love. All spiritual failure is failure primarily in love. To be lost is to be lost to love. And increased agape love is the only thing that will unite the Church.

Love Never Fails

The gifts of the Spirit are important, but there is something more important. For instance, prophecy, which is based on conceptual truth, is important. We are urged to "despise not prophesyings" (1 Thess. 5:20). But the gift of prophecy is not *all important*. "Whether there be prophesies, they shall fail" (1 Cor. 13:8): we will not need prophesies in heaven. But *love never fails*. Tongues are important, but they are not *all important*. "Whether there be tongues, they shall cease" (1 Cor. 13:8): we will not need the gift of tongues in heaven. But *love never fails*. The gift of knowledge is important, but it is not *all important*. "Whether there be knowledge, it shall vanish away" (1 Cor. 13:8): we will not need the gift of knowledge in heaven. But *love never fails*. Agape love, not gifts that will vanish, is the basis of rank and authority in that future kingdom. Love is the most powerful force in the universe. Otherwise God would not be God, for "God is love" (1 John 4:8). Satan did not know this or he would not have rebelled. Satan's rebellion was against agape love. Is it possible that we have been deceived and have joined in his rebellion against love? He apparently believed that omnipotence is vested in brute force and all the works of the flesh, instead of in love. He evidently persuaded one-third of the population of heaven. But he and they have *lost*—because love is the ultimate power in the universe. All who are influenced by Satan's viewpoint risk eternal loss.

The Only Uniting Factor—Agape Love

Correct doctrine, right views of conceptual truth, can never unite the Body of Christ because fallen minds can never be absolutely sure that their positions are infallible. "Now I know in part" (1 Cor. 13:12). That means that error may dilute our concepts. Therefore the Church cannot unite on that platform. There is one basis and *only one* on which the Body of Christ can ever unite, and that is *more love...agape love.* Repeating, no breach in the Body of Christ is ever caused by superior knowledge, differing convictions, or divergent views of truth but only by *lack of agape love.* These may be the occasion of the breach, but not the cause.

The person who does not speak in tongues but who excels in agape love will accept and fellowship with one who does speak in tongues. They are members of the same family. Sufficient love and reverence for God will unite them. The person who speaks in tongues and who also excels in agape love will accept and fellowship with one who doesn't speak in tongues. They are also members of the same family. Sufficient love will cover their differences. Agape love is the only thing that will unite them.

The Essence of Truth—Agape Love

To major on conceptual truth instead of agape love is actually to forfeit the essence of truth, for *the essence of truth is agape love.* Truth is a person. "I am the truth" (John 14:6). That person is also love. "God is love" (1 John 4:8). Things that equal the same thing equal each other. Therefore, *error flourishes most in the absence of agape love. Agape love and only agape love is a guarantor of truth,* and is the only thing that unites the Body.

Also, agape love is the only guarantor of truth because it is the only guarantor of total objectivity, total honesty, total freedom from bias and prejudice. Agape love is the only thing that delivers from self-interest, self-centeredness and self-love. All or any of these are certain to corrupt, distort, and falsify all views of truth. *For this reason, agape love and only agape love is a guarantor of truth.* Scholarship is considered the means, the process, the technique by which truth is discovered, verified and communicated. But scholarship which ignores the importance, necessity and relevance of agape love is suspect, deficient and ineffectual. *Therefore, agape love is an essential ingredient to genuine scholarship.* I consider this one of the most important concepts in this book.

To major on conceptual truth and make it a criterion of fellowship is to rend the Body since "we know in part only." To major in *agape love* is to heal and unite because *love covers* and, if permitted, like a rising flood, wipes out every wall of separation and division. Agape love unites because it encompasses, embraces, and transcends all truth. Therefore, "let love be your greatest [supreme] aim" (1 Cor. 14:1 *LB*).

Only One Power

To this present day, with few exceptions, the Church has failed to comprehend that agape love is the ultimate and therefore the supreme power in the universe. Jesus said, "All power is given unto me in heaven and in earth" (Matt. 28:18). If this is literally true, there is only one power in the universe. So far as universal cosmic intelligence is concerned, power that is not permanent is not power at all, even while it masquerades as such. This is the way God sees it because He lives in eternity and sees things from the eternal standpoint. Viewed from an eternal standpoint, power that is not permanent is already destroyed. Therefore, every thought, word, plan, purpose, motive or action that does not originate in and operate by agape love is counterproductive. It ingests the seeds of its own destruction. *Any work or ministry that is built and maintained by any other method than agape love, any religious success that is achieved or promoted by anything else, is therefore false, fading and illusory. Such "labor for God" is only shadow boxing.*

The Only Redeeming Force

Agape love is the only redeeming force in the universe. With apologies to Emmet Fox, the following is a paraphrase of his inspiring panegyric on love:

There is no difficulty that enough agape love
will not conquer;
No disease that enough agape love will not heal;
No door that enough agape love will not open;
No gulf that enough agape love will not bridge;
No wall that enough agape love will not throw
down;
No sin that enough agape love will not redeem.

It makes no difference how deeply seated may
be the trouble; how hopeless the outlook; how
muddled the tangle; how great the mistake. A
sufficient realization of agape love will dissolve
it all.... If only you could love enough you
would be the happiest and most powerful being
in the world.

9

JUDGMENTALISM

Judgmentalism Defined

Jesus said, "Judge not" (Matthew 7:1).

"Brothers, do not slander one another Anyone who speaks against his brother, or judges him, speaks against the law and judges it. When you judge the law, you are not keeping it, but sitting in judgment on it. There is only one Law-giver and Judge, one who is able to save and destroy. But you—who are you to judge your neighbor?" (James 4:11-12 *NIV*).

"Therefore, let us stop passing judgment on one another" (Rom. 14:13 *NIV*).

"Accept one another, then, just as Christ accepted you, in order to bring praise to God" (Rom. 15:7 *NIV*).

Judgmentalism may be defined nontechnically as unfavorable judgment, criticism, or condemnation of others because of their conduct or supposed erroneous beliefs, wrong motives, or character. It is an arbitrary evaluation of another person's worth. In the realm of religion it often results in the rejection of a person because of his opinion in nonessentials to salvation. It is the most frequent cause of division and fragmentation of the Body of Christ.

Disunity probably causes more souls to be lost than any other sin. Therefore, we may someday discover that *the love that covers,* that prefers and honors one another, that wipes out judgmentalism and unites the Body of Christ, *is a greater miracle than opening blind eyes, deaf ears, or healing the lame "so that they leap as an hart,"* or any other sensational or prodigious sign or wonder.

This does not mean that opening blind eyes and deaf ears and healing the lame is unimportant. It does mean that the love that unites the Body is *more important.* "Now abideth faith [that works miracles], hope [that makes us happy], love [that unites the Body], these three; but the greatest of these is love" (1 Cor. 13:13, *New Scofield*).

If salvation of a soul is the greatest miracle, then the love that unites the Body and releases the Spirit and paves the way for the salvation of souls may be at least a close second. *It may be, therefore, that striving for and featuring spectacular types of miracles is less important than seeking Body unity.*

Lucifer's Syndrome

One cannot become judgmental without elevating himself—and self-elevation is Lucifer's syndrome. It caused his fall and all of the sin and sorrow that followed in its wake. Satan could not be content to be second even to God Himself. He has infected the human race with this virus. The mother tincture or essence of a fallen condition is self-exaltation, self-promotion, the determination to be first. This is what triggered Satan's rebellion and the first broken fellowships in heaven. It may be, therefore, that the disposition of self-effacement, which is being willing to humble oneself and be last instead of first, is a greater miracle than walking on water. We would become ecstatic if we witnessed someone walking on water. We would consider him worthy of high honor. *We may someday discover that a greater miracle and one requiring more supernatural power to work in us is lowliness of mind and the love that covers, heals breaches, and unites the Body—far greater than any demonstration of the sensational gifts that can tempt us to pride and self-glory.*

It is because too many of us want to be first and too few of us are willing to be last, or even second, that the Body remains broken and the hands of the Holy Spirit tied. *May it not be that the supreme miracle—the miracle of all miracles of the Church age—is the love that covers, the love that is willing to be last that the Body may be united and the Holy Spirit released?*

The Supreme Miracle

The Body made one, as Jesus is one with the Father: every member "made perfect in one" with each other and the Godhead—this is the unanswered heart cry of Jesus in John 17. *The absolute unity of the Body would be the supreme miracle of the Church age, not only because it overcomes human division, malice and malevolence (which is the hallmark of the fall) but because, as Jesus said, it is the most convincing testimony to the world that God has invaded the human scene.* "That they all may be one, as thou, Father, art in me, and I in thee, that they also may be one in us; *that the world may believe that thou hast sent me"* (John 17:21).

Unity, love for one another, according to Jesus, is the *one thing* that proves discipleship to the world. "By this shall all men know that ye are my disciples, if ye have love one to another" (John 13:35). *Unity is the one thing that authenticates Christ's divinity and overcomes the world's unbelief.* Unbelief is the chief sin of the world. It is the sin which dooms all lost souls. This is why the love that covers, that heals and unites the Body, is the supreme miracle of the Church age, and the lack of it the chief sin of the Church. *The supreme miracle of unity of the Body would release the Holy Spirit in a world-wide revival of the miraculous that would dwarf all previous demonstrations and usher in an ingathering of souls around the world in unprecedented proportions. Only the unity of the Body can produce the real "latter rain" for which we pray.*

Judgmentalism Always Wrong

When will we learn that judgmentalism is a sin, a direct violation of Jesus' command given in Matthew 7:1? A clear indication that judgmentalism is always wrong is that *it always, without exception, dims one's relationship with God and interferes with one's prayer life.* One cannot pray effectively for others while he is judging and condemning them. Lovelessness slays the spirit of prayer because prayer for others is inspired only by a loving concern. Can love and judgmental controversy dwell in the same heart at the same time? *Difference of opinion may; but personal resentment, irritation, and offense will stifle the love that covers.* Personal respect includes also respect for each other's opinions. This could avoid broken fellowships and Body division.

Judgmentalism—the Beam

There is no prohibition against judging one's self (1 Cor. 11:31) but we are specifically forbidden to judge others (Matt. 7:1-5, James 4:11-12, Rom. 14:13). In the parable of the mote and the beam (following His injunction against judging others) Jesus is saying *that the vice of judgmentalism is itself worse than the fault that evokes it.* If we understand Jesus correctly, *judgmentalism is the "beam in the eye" that prevents clear vision to remove the mote from the brother's eye.*

Satan's Method

Only nonessentials to salvation can divide the Body because the true Church agrees on all beliefs necessary to salvation. Without such essential beliefs, no group can qualify as part of the real Body of Christ. *Therefore, all division in the true Church must be over nonessentials.* When conflicting opinions arise in nonessentials and cannot be reconciled, what is the scriptural course of action? There are two options: One is to resort to lobbying; that is, to political action, pressure and wire-pulling to promote the preferred view. This usually results in controversy which gives rise to increased judgmentalism and more broken fellowships. This is always inspired by Satan and aggravates and compounds the breach. *To resort to judgmentalism is always wrong because Christ has forbidden it: "Judge not."*

God's Method

There is another method...and the only one that is effective. It is God's way. If a wrong has been done or a wrong decision has been made which threatens division, is God aware of it? If I know a thing is wrong and needs to be corrected, is it possible that an all-wise God does not? If God knows that an injustice has been done, that a wrong decision has been made that threatens harm, is He not as sincerely interested in its correction as I? *Since His way is the only way to correct it, how will He do it and what does He desire of us?*

Prayer Is Where the Action Is

If a wrong decision has been made, *only God can correct it.* Human interference by judgmentalism or party spirit always fails, for that originates with Satan and is sure to exacerbate and aggravate the crisis. Because Christ has forbidden it—because He has said, "Judge not"—*all judgmentalism has to be satanically inspired. Therefore, the only way that any wrong situation, any situation which Satan has spawned, can be corrected is not by more judgmentalism but by prayer, for prayer is where the action is.* Jack Taylor has said, "Prayer is the only thing that Satan cannot handle."[5]

Because God devised the plan of prayer primarily as on-the-job training for the Church in overcoming Satan in preparation for rulership in the ages to come, *He does nothing in the affairs of earth except through her prayers.* If He by-passed the Church and did the things He wants done without her cooperation in prayer, she would never learn overcoming. *That is why God does nothing in earthly affairs except through prayer.*[6]

An Official Decree

Even though all authority in heaven and in earth was given to Jesus (Matt. 28:18), *He has vested this hard-won authority over Satan in the members of His Body.* Luke 10:19 records this: "Behold, I give you power [authority]...over all the power of the enemy; and nothing shall by any means hurt you." Once this power and authority was exercised by angels. According to Revelation 12, when Lucifer led a revolt in heaven, it was Michael and his angels who actually confronted and forcefully expelled Lucifer and his angels. "And there was war in heaven, Michael and his angels fought against the dragon, and the dragon and his angels fought back. But he was not strong enough, and they lost their place in heaven. The great dragon was hurled down—that ancient serpent called the devil or Satan, who leads the whole world astray. He was hurled to the earth, and his angels with him" (Rev. 12:7-9 *NIV*).

From this account it appears that the Godhead was not directly and personally involved in this encounter. Although all power and authority resides in Them, evidently for this purpose power was delegated to Michael and his angels *and they became God's surrogates or deputies, His enforcement agency.* In Luke 10, Jesus alludes to Satan's expulsion: "I beheld Satan fall like lightning from heaven." Then He continues, 'Behold I give you power [authority]...over all the power of the enemy." *The authority which once the angels exercised, Jesus now delegated to the members of His Body on earth. This is a sweeping, official, constitutional, governmental decree charged with all the authority of heaven.*

Additional Confirmation

This view is further substantiated and proved conclusively by Paul's statement in Ephesians 2:4-6 *NIV,* "But because of his great love for us, God, who is rich in mercy, made us alive with Christ even when we were dead in transgressions...and raised us up with Christ and *seated us* with him in the heavenly realms in Christ Jesus" (emphasis mine). Dimension does not apply in the realm of the Spirit as it does in the material realm. Distance does not have the same validity in the spiritual as in the physical or material. Because this is true, my spirit (my real person) can be joined with God's Spirit while my body is on earth. The fact that God does nothing in earthly affairs apart from the prayers and faith of His Church, the members of His Body, verifies, demonstrates, and gives substance to the understanding that the Church has already been raised and, at this moment, is seated with Christ in the heavenlies. In *Destined for the Throne,* it is declared that while God in heaven sovereignly makes all decisions governing earthly affairs, He has placed the full responsibility and authority for the implementation, enforcement, and administration of those decisions squarely upon the shoulders of His Church (page 46). An additional scriptural basis for this declaration is found in Matthew 16:17-19 *NIV*: "Jesus replied, 'Blessed are you, Simon son of Jonah, for this was not revealed to you by man, but by my Father in heaven. And I tell you that you are Peter, and on this rock I will build my church, and the gates of Hades will not overcome it. I will give unto you the keys of the kingdom of heaven; whatever you bind on earth will be bound in heaven, and whatever you loose on earth will be loosed in heaven.' " Also in Matthew 18:18 *NIV*: "I tell you the truth, whatever you bind on earth will be bound in heaven...." According to John 20:21-23 *NIV*, a similar principle was repeated after the resurrection: "Again Jesus said, 'Peace be with you! As the Father has sent me, I am sending you.' And with that he breathed on them and said, 'Receive the Holy Spirit. If you forgive anyone his sins, they are forgiven; if you do not forgive them, they are not forgiven.' "

These passages of Scripture confirm the truth of the resurrection and enthronement of the Church with Christ and *constitute her a full partner with Christ in the government of earth*. This in no sense interferes with or alters God's sovereignty, since all decisions are made sovereignly in heaven.

Limited to the Body

To use another biblical figure, as the organic Head of the Body, Christ has voluntarily delegated the exercise of His authority on earth to His Church. It is hers and hers *alone*. She is His hands and feet. She is Heaven's enforcement agency. *Although all power and authority originates exclusively in Christ, it appears that since His ascension and the birth of the Church, He chooses to exercise this authority over Satan in earthly affairs only through the Church, His Body, because this is the only way she learns overcoming* (*Destined for the Throne*, page 49).

Judgmentalism Paralyzes the Spirit of Prayer

We have seen that all Body divisions are spawned in hell and promoted by Satan, largely through judgmentalism. Therefore judgmentalism, which is Satan's tool and originates with him, can never heal any breach that he manufactures. That would be like Satan casting out Satan. *The only power that can bind and cast out Satan and repair damage done by judgmentalism is supernatural power, the power of the Holy Spirit.* By God's own choice, that power is released only by the prayers of the Church—and judgmentalism always paralyzes the spirit of prayer.

Satan's Trap

Because authority over Satan in earthly affairs has been delegated to the Church as His Body, Christ Himself exercises no authority in mundane affairs over Satan and his hierarchy except through her prayer and faith. When a satanically inspired controversy arises in the Body, it can never be settled by lapsing into loveless judgmentalism. All judgmentalism is of the devil and therefore can never heal any Body problem. Therefore, the only successful approach to such problems is the approach of believing prayer, *because prayer is where the action is.* Where *the love that covers* prevails, Satan's tools and techniques will be rejected and prayer will supplant carnal methods. Where agape love prevails, believing prayer will make possible the exercise of God-given authority over Satan and his hierarchy. When he is bound and cast out by united prayer and faith, *division will be overcome, wounds will be healed, the Body will be united, the world will be convinced, sinners will be saved, and Christ will be glorified. Prayer, not judgmentalism, is where the action is.* Where *the love that covers* prevails and the Church chooses the option of prayer instead of judgmentalism, it always demonstrates that *prayer is where the action is*. Any group or communion which practices this theology will discover that it works. If the prayer approach does not solve the problem, the trouble may be in the spirit of the pray-er himself rather than the approach. It could be that something in his life is hindering the effectiveness of prayer. *If prayer does not remedy the situation, it is certain that nothing will.* Therefore, do not fall into Satan's trap of judgmentalism. Choose God's way, *the love that covers. Love never fails.* This passage means that love's resources are always all-sufficient.

10

THE MOST URGENT PROBLEM OF THE CHURCH

The Scandal of the Ages

Disunity in the Body of Christ is the scandal of the ages. *I believe that it is the most heinous and destructive sin of the Church.* This fact seems to have escaped the attention of the Church until this hour. The seriousness of this sin appears not only in John 17 and the Johannine Epistles, but also in Paul's instructions concerning the Lord's Supper in 1 Corinthians 11. In 11:18, Paul says, "In the first place, I hear that when you come together as a church, there are divisions among you." Paul's instructions can be understood only in the context of division and lack of fellowship: "For as you eat, each of you goes ahead without waiting for anybody else" (1 Cor. 11:21 *NIV*).

In verses 27-30, Paul says, "Therefore, whosoever eats this bread or drinks the cup of the Lord in an unworthy manner will be guilty of sinning against the body and blood of the Lord. A man ought to examine himself before he eats of the bread and drinks of the cup. For anyone who eats and drinks without recognizing [the unity of] the body of the Lord eats and drinks judgment upon himself. That is why many of you are weak and sick, and a number of you have fallen asleep" (*NIV*).

The unity of the Body of Christ is evidently in view

because of the preceding context concerning division. This indicates that the words "without recognizing" (*NIV*) or "not discerning" (*KJV*) the Lord's body refer to the failure of the believer to recognize the unity of the Church viewed as the corporate Body of Christ (See *The Wycliffe Bible Commentary*). To fail to recognize, understand, appreciate and preserve the unity of the Body of Christ on earth is the equivalent of reopening the wounds of the Savior on the cross. Paul is saying that the wounding of Christ's corporate Body brings Him similar pain as the wounding of His fleshly body on the cross. Eating the bread and drinking the wine while perpetuating broken fellowships, without first healing and restoring unity in the Body, is to bring judgment upon the worshiper, resulting in sickness and sometimes even death. I see no conflict between this and the conventional interpretation of this passage. If this interpretation of the Scriptures by *The Wycliffe Bible Commentary* is correct, it emphasizes and stresses the magnitude and seriousness of the sin of disunity. *It is sinning against the Body and blood of the Lord.* John 17 throbs with the very longing of Jesus' heart for this unity. *The unity of the Body is probably the most urgent problem of the Church today,* as in all ages past. The greatest obstacle to the salvation of the world may not be the sinfulness of the world itself *but the sin of disunity in the Church.* If judgment is to be avoided, the solution of this problem can no longer be ignored.

The Greatest Hindrance
What and where is the greatest hindrance to unity?

Many feel that it is not primarily among the laity, because in general they seem more open to efforts to foster fellowship. If this is true, could it be possible that the greatest obstacle to unity is among the clergy, the spiritual leaders of the church? Now we are not thinking of liberal, modernistic, and humanistic propagandists. We are thinking of conservative Bible-believing evangelicals—preachers, evangelists, administrators and leaders. We are referring to men who are considered mature, men of large spiritual stature, even deeply spiritual men, including those of world-wide reputation. *How few there are who have comprehended the importance to God of the unity of His Body.* Has not the Church, including its most revered pastors, evangelists, teachers, theologians and administrators, too long ignored and discounted the importance of Jesus' intense longing expressed in John 17? Is it possible that the answer to Christ's prayer is delayed by ostensible spiritual leaders?

The Crowning Achievement

In addition to the reason previously given—that disunity probably causes more souls to be lost than any other sin—there is another important reason why it is so crucial to God. It is for the same reason that unity is important in *any* family. Any worthy parent is distressed by strife, friction, hostility, to say nothing of other evidences of lovelessness among members of his household. *The parent loves every member equally.* When one member threatens the well-being of another, *the parent feels as truly threatened as the child.* The one who poses the threat will not forfeit the love of the parent but he will forfeit his approval. For the same reason, *our heavenly Father is painfully sensitive to the unloving attitude of the members of His family toward one another. Strife in His family is infinitely more distressing to Him than to an earthly parent because His love for each of His children is infinitely greater. He loves all of them with equal compassion.* This is one reason why unity is so important to God and why His children's attitude toward one another is of such great concern to Him. To learn this lesson and adopt this life-principle of *love for every member of God's family* may be the crowning achievement of one's spiritual life and career.

The First Step

What is the first step toward the healing of the wounds of Christ's Body? It may be the recognition and acknowledgement of the enormity and the heinousness of this sin. The next step is sincere repentance: "If my people, who are called by my name, will humble themselves and pray and seek my face and turn from their wicked ways, then will I hear from heaven and will forgive their sin and will heal their land" (2 Chron. 7:14 *NIV*).

The "wicked ways" of the Church, the Body of Christ, from which God's people must repent do not consist primarily of impurity, vice, crime, and physical violence. They are our unloving attitudes toward one another, revealed by our critical judgment and broken fellowships. These are the "wicked ways" among the Lord's people which require repentance. More than anything else, this disunity is preventing real revival and the Lord's return.

Revival always begins in the best people first. If spiritual leaders will lead the way in humbling, confession and repentance, the rank and file will follow. It is usually not they who insist on promoting and maintaining division. Is it possible that those with vested interests are most responsible for the continued brokenness of Christ's Body? Is it possible that Jesus is being "wounded in the house of [His best] friends"? (Zech. 13:6).

The illusion that congregations and denominations can be built and held together only by divisive methods must be forever abandoned. Ecclesiastical leaders, administrators, theologians, writers and propagandists, and all others with vested interest, must cease to aid, abet and sanctify division. Religio-political ambitions must not continue to overshadow spiritual values by fostering divisive policies. Success, gauged largely by growth in numbers and finance and rewarded by political and financial advancement, must yield to a larger vision of a united Body.

The Crux of the Matter

Does anyone deny the existence of such unworthy financial and political ambitions in the great and not so great ecclesiastical organizations today? Here lies the crux of the matter. The focus is on this question, Will ecclesiastical authorities, administrators and leaders, including pastors and evangelists, be able to comprehend this dilemma and lead the way to its resolution? *Or will they continue to be guilty of the Body and blood of the Lord?* No individual can answer for another *but each can deliver his own soul by offering fellowship to all who are born again, regardless of theological differences.* "For anyone who eats and drinks without recognizing [the unity of] the body of the Lord eats and drinks judgment upon himself. That is why many of you are weak and sick, and a number of you have fallen asleep" (1 Cor. 11:29-30 *NIV*).

Can Repentance Come Too Late?

Repentance can come too late, and the so-called spiritual leaders may be the first to suffer rapidly approaching judgment. The cliche "It is later than you think" may be more ominous than we realize. With all due respect to the Gallop polls, atheism, Communism, Mohammedanism, Oriental mysticism, occultism and the various false cults—all are intensely anti-Christ and are increasing more rapidly than the Christian faith. *The growth of the heathen population in the world far outstrips the growth of the Church.* After 1900 years, the Christian faith is still a minority faith, an island in a sea of hostility. Humanism, secularism, atheism and false cults are making impressive gains. Communism continues its expansion with frightening speed. Some of the best-informed military minds believe that the die has already been cast and that the Communist policy of *external encirclement plus internal demoralization plus nuclear blackmail...leading to progressive surrender, has already passed the point of no return.* No longer is it plausible to say, "It can't happen here."

It May Happen Here

In his November 1, 1979 *Newsletter,* Dr. Fred Schwarz, founder and President of the Christian Anti-

Communist Crusade, carried a description of a fund-raising rally under the leadership of Bob Avakian, Chairman of the Revolutionary Communist Party within the USA, a radical Maoist group. The rally was reported in the Los Angeles Times by Reporter Bella Stumbo. Extracts from Stumbo's description of the rally follows:

"How many of you would gladly smash that color TV of yours over the head of a pig in order to make revolution?" he screeched to a crowd of about 300 Party faithfuls packed into an auditorium at Convention Center earlier this month. A sea of eager hands immediately shot up. And that was only the beginning.

By the time Avakian was finished three hours later, most of his audience—racially mixed, mostly under 30 and mostly blue collar—looked dazed or crazed enough to rush out and at least hock the TV, along with their clothes and maybe their cars, in order to raise the $1 million that Avakian told them the Party needs....

"I mean, we won't kill some dumb jerk just because he jumped us for passing out our paper," Avakian qualified. "He can probably be reeducated. But it's another story with these hired thugs and killers like the police...and the leaders of this country, like Mr. Carter!"

The crowd cheered.

Avakian ended with a shrill, chilling vision of masses of murderous workers, "millions strong," rushing through the streets of America, armed, shooting every "blood-sucking, boot-licking capital-ist" in sight.

After Avakian's speech, several Party members rushed forward to pledge their loyalty.

One emotion-choked postal worker rose to tell "a beautiful story" about his four-year-old daughter.

"The other day, she asked me why so many peo-ple were poor," he said softly. "So I told her because the capitalists take away their money. And do you know what she said?" He paused, swallowing.

"She said, 'Then we should kill the capitalists.' "

That brought down the house. Several people vowed on the spot to pledge weekly or monthly donations in the name of their children.

Some people had been so excited at the prospect of hearing Avakian in person that they brought their babies along.

"This dude is the greatest revolutionary leader alive. He is one dangerous cat—and I just wanted the kid to pick up his vibes," explained one such parent, a bearded boy in blue jeans, wearing a feisty little workers' cap.

The *Kiplinger Letter*

The *Kiplinger Washington Letter* of March 24, 1978, states, "By 1981 or 1982, Russia would have superiority over the U.S....under this arrangement [the Salt II treaty]. That is what U.S. Intelligence people foresee. The Soviets would have a missile strength so deep they could retaliate even after a missile strike by the U.S. They could hit us a second time. Probably they wouldn't need to. *The mere threat of another major blow might easily do the trick. In fact, the knowledge of such Red power could be sufficient to cause the U.S. to knuckle under...without a fight."*

Mideast Oil

Under the headline, "Soviets Seek Mideast Oil Control," Larry Peterson, Staff writer for the Orange County *Register,* quotes Vladimir Sakharov, an ex-KGB agent and consular official. In an address to the World Affairs Council of Orange County, California, given and reported on January 16, 1981, Sakharov claims that the cornerstone of the Soviet Middle East policy has been manipulation of major supplies of oil in an attempt to destabilize the economies of the Western World.

The current Russian initiatives, he said, stem from a twenty-year plan devised in 1965.

As a part of the plan and related programs, he said, the Russians took over South Yemen, fomented turmoil in Iran, invaded Afghanistan, made major inroads in Libya, Syria, Algeria, and provoked war between Iraq and Iran. He said the Soviets' plans to dominate the oil-rich peninsula are developing "just marvelously."

Vulnerability of U.S.

Today the shadow of the Kremlin looms ever darker over the world. It has been reported that General George Keegan, former Chief of Air Force Intelligence, said: "If [the Soviet Union] attacks, it is my judgment that 160 million Americans would die in one night and that no more than five million Russians could be killed in response.

"And with nerve gas now being produced in tens of thousands of tons a year, in violation of a treaty which the Soviet Union induced 85 nations, including the U.S., to sign...we have dismantled our capability to defend ourselves and the Soviets find themselves in a position of absolute advantage over the world. If the Soviets should choose at the same time to attack our navy and the fleets of our allies, it would be all over within one week; and within three additional weeks, every cargo ship of the Free World at sea could be sent to the bottom of the ocean—so superior are the Soviets."

Today, the entire world is "holding its breath," waiting for the crack of doom.

Religious Leaders Catalogued

Our hope is in Ezekiel 38...but the signs of Communist aggression continue to multiply. Afghanistan is not the last. In every country which has fallen to the Communists, the religious community is the first to suffer. It is common knowledge that in most nations overrun by the Communists, religious leaders have been catalogued in advance and, should they refuse to be "re-educated" and resist cooperation, have been imprisoned, tortured and slain. Some intelligence reports indicate that the U.S. is no exception and that its religious leaders are already scheduled for seizure. In recent news, Senator Barry Goldwater is quoted as saying that the Chinese Communists murdered at least 50 million people in their rise to power. Under Pol Pot and his successors, typical Communists, almost an entire nation (Cambodia) has been practically wiped out.

Other untold millions have died and multitudes are still perishing daily in Russia, Vietnam, Ethiopia, Afghanistan and in every Communist-conquered nation in the world.

Is it possible that this is the only way the answer to Jesus' prayer in John 17 can be realized? Is persecution the only means by which God can bring together both spiritual leaders and the Church in general? Is it the only thing that will deliver from unholy ambition and carnal strife? Only a mighty supernatural revival of *agape love* can turn the tide. Only a monumental, earth-shaking revival of repentance, confession, restitution and brokenness can bring the desired end.

A Dreadful Alternative

Because Communism is demon-inspired, the only force that can successfully challenge its advance is supernatural power. And the only way that sufficient spiritual power can be generated and released is by the combined prayers of a united Body. Many believe that the handwriting is already on the wall and that this is no phony cry of "wolf." A world-wide conspiracy, masterminded by Satan himself, has prepared the way for Antichrist. Satan still seems to believe that he will yet dethrone the Almighty, and believe it or not, *disunity is his most successful tool.* "It is later than you think" is more than an empty cliche. "The night is far spent, the day is at hand" (Rom. 13:12). That is, the "Day of the Lord" foretold by saints, seers and prophets of ages past. *Is the Church and its spiritual leaders so insensitive to Christ's prayer, so wedded to their own worldly aims and ambitions, that the only thing that will accomplish the answer to Christ's prayer for the unity of His Body is the actual revelation of the Man of Sin? When the Antichrist appears, will he find the Church still helplessly broken and bleeding from internal strife over nonessentials? The only alternative to loving one's brother may be execution by the Antichrist.*

A Personal Responsibility

Perhaps some are saying that the unity of the Body is an "impossible dream"; that Jesus' prayer will never be answered. To most it seems that way. Be that as it may, each one is responsible for himself alone. Only as each accepts that responsibility can the "impossible dream" come true. Only as each is willing to cease idolatry, to cease worshiping his own opinions in nonessentials; only as each reaches maturity in *agape love,* the love for Jesus Himself which surpasses self-adulation and worship masquerading under the illusion of "loyalty to truth"—only then will Jesus' prayer be fulfilled. It is as simple as that. *What are you going to do with the prayer that Jesus prayed?*

Maranatha!

[1]There are three Greek words that are translated "love": *eros*—the love between the sexes; *philos*—the love of friendship; and *agape*—the love which is the essence of God Himself. "God is love" (1 John 4:8).

[2]J. I. Packer, *Evangelism and the Sovereignty of God* (Inter-Varsity Press, Chicago, IL, 1961), pp.18-19.

[3]*Maclaren's Expositions, The Gospel of St. Matthew, Chapters 9-18* (Hodder and Stoughton, London, 1892), pp.352-374.

[4]George Otis, *The Thunder of His Power* (Bible Voice, Van Nuys, CA 91409, 1978).

[5]Jack Taylor, *Life's Limitless Reach* (Broadman, Nashville, TN, 1977).

[6]Paul E. Billheimer, *Destined for the Throne* (Christian Literature Crusade, Ft. Washington, PA 19034, 1975), Chapter 3, "The Mystery of Prayer."

[7]George C. Watson, *A Pot of Oil* (Newby Book Room, Jamestown, NC 27282, no date).

EPILOGUE

A Spiritual Odyssey

I was born and reared in a time when speaking in tongues was not only unacceptable, in most circles it was anathema. Many devout, saintly people considered this practice not only error but actual heresy. To some it was even demonic. Their prejudice was so deeply seated and massive that you were considered to be in complete disgrace if you associated with those speaking in tongues, much less attended one of their services. Until recently this attitude has been very common among many non-Pentecostal groups and seems still to persist in some areas.

Although I was never fully convinced that the above appraisal was justified, I still felt the restraint of serious and sober warnings that were given to me during my early ministry as a teenager. However, in more mature years, when literature on the Pentecostal movement came to my hands, I began to see, and openly took the position, that if God had His way all the gifts of the Spirit would be present and exercised in the Church today in a similar proportion as in the early Church. It was a joyful surprise to me when I began to meet various Pentecostal people who seemed to be sane, intelligent, and spiritually rational. I was further overjoyed to find some with beautiful testimonies of transforming grace that had resulted in normal, well-balanced and apparently mature Christian character. Further study of Pentecostal authors brought me increasing understanding and blessing. But although my prejudice began to melt, a barrier still remained.

After *Destined for the Throne* began to circulate I received an invitation from a Charismatic ministry to participate in a Conference on the Holy Spirit. Following investigation and prayer I accepted. Although I felt awkward at times in this association, there was such openness to the message of prayer and such spontaneous expression of love and acceptance that I found it increasingly possible to adjust.

When I was invited to a teaching position on a Charismatic television network, although I knew I risked being ecclesiastically declassed I gave it consideration. I was received with open arms, experiencing sincere fellowship and agape love. But in spite of this, increased adjustment became necessary. Notwithstanding the warm, sympathetic and enthusiastic reception of my message, so deep-seated were my reservations that, by the end of the first year of my television ministry, I was in deep inner trouble. I found myself in a wholly new religious culture which was difficult to evaluate. While learning from and deeply appreciating much in the fellowship, I was unable to avoid falling into a judgmentalism which threatened my ability to continue in that ministry.

Under these circumstances God, in His mercy, began a new discipline in my life. After this first year of much inner conflict, I suffered a severe intestinal infection which continued unabated for a full month. Consulting a Christian physician and following his advice and medication brought only temporary relief. The possible end of my entire ministry clearly was at hand. During this month of suffering I earnestly sought the Lord. Following Maclaren's suggestion that "every affliction comes with a message from the heart of God," day after day I humbled myself and sought to hear God's voice. Not until I was overwhelmed with desperation did I become quiet enough inside to receive even a hint of God's word to me. The voice of the flesh was so strident that it stifled the still, small voice of God.

When I became sufficiently quiet inwardly, the Spirit zeroed in on my judgmentalism. As I waited upon the Lord, increasing light dawned and I began to repent. Immediately my infection decreased and soon disappeared, never to return. I was compelled to accept this as an indication that my judgmentalism had itself been judged by God. Thus I was able to continue my ministry and association with this group.

Unreasonable as it was, traces of my prejudice persisted. Through this experience, however, God made it clear, to my satisfaction, that the Lord Himself had indeed brought me to this place and that I should not allow prejudice to interfere. Through the discipline of this affliction and restoration I became convinced, not only that God had definitely brought me to this work, but that despite my reservations, God Himself had raised up this ministry and was using it to His glory.

Yet I found it difficult to accept and adjust to people who had been reared and conditioned in this culture. Although God had delivered me from a certain amount of prejudice against the culture in general, I found it difficult to avoid judgment of individuals in particular, especially those who seemed to indulge in extremes. This was so persistent that it continued to pose a disturbing handicap to my ministry. A few months after my restoration from the intestinal infection, I awakened during the night with a distressing heart problem. This problem had surfaced in previous years when I had suffered massive stress and fatigue from overwork and loss of sleep. For six weeks this problem continued unabated in an intensified form, again threatening an end to my ministry. Consultation with a Christian physician yielded no relief.

Again I was driven to God. During these six weeks I joined the Psalmist in his prayer, "Search me, O God, and know my heart; try me, and know my thoughts; and see if there be any wicked way in me, and lead me in the way everlasting" (Psalm 139:23-24).

This experience was no picnic. These were perplexing days, days of deep heart searching and self-humbling. Although my ministry had covered a span of more than sixty-five years, I now faced a devastating crisis. Inner stillness does not come easily. After many weeks of waiting upon God, I was again brought face to face with my prejudice and judgmentalism that, in spite of former chastening, I recognized as stubbornly persisting. Figuratively speaking God had taken "hammer and tongs" to me. I cannot understand the process. Gradually the conviction grew in my spirit that my deep-seated judgmental attitude was grieving God. As I began to recognize this and repent, lo, the heart problem vanished. Out of this experience came an entirely new revelation of the sin of judgmentalism, of which a portrayal appears in Chapter 9 of this volume.

Evidently this was not sufficient. The disease was virulent and of long standing. I did not know how unrea-

soning, intolerant and deep-seated my bias was. God
had to do a totally new thing in my life. I am convinced
that I have many brothers and sisters in non-
Pentecostal ranks who suffer the same qualms.
Although God had dealt so specifically with me, rem-
nants of misgivings remained. God's patience must
have been sorely tried. After a clear demonstration of
God's guidance, so unreconstructed were my inhibi-
tions that I continued to feel like an outsider. My deliverance apparently called for further measures. God
dealt with me this time through my wife's affliction.

Shortly before our departure for an important series
of engagements, she was stricken with severe, disabling
arthritic back pain. We wondered if this was God's way
of informing us that this trip was not His will. We gave
this due consideration, but she was fully convinced that
we must go, even if she had to go in a wheel chair. Her
trouble continued intermittently through the entire series and became even more acute after our return. For
more than a week she was unable to lie on the bed and
was compelled to lie in a reclining chair day and night.

During all of this time we were in much anxiety,
frustration, grief and pain. We were mystified, baffled
and broken. We spent many hours seeking to discover
our fault. God took us deeper and deeper in self-
emptying, humbling, and self-repudiation. We
explored every possible angle. Only when we reached
direst extremity did we finally arrive at the place of
utter stillness and deliverance from the activity of the
old nature. After many days and nights of severe suffering and pain, God spoke.

I cannot fully explain how it came. But from deep

within my chastened spirit a voice arose so soft, so unobtrusive, so quiet and still that it was scarcely discernable. During our morning prayers at the time of greatest extremity, the one thing that began to impinge upon my consciousness was "the outsider" syndrome. I grasped it like a drowning man reaching for a straw. *And it held. It became tangible.* During our devotions that morning, I talked it all out with God. I poured it out in confession and repentance. And my wife followed suit. When we finished, lo and behold, that very day the excruciating spasms and severe back pain vanished. That night she retired to her bed. She has slept well ever since.

What do you think? How would you explain this? Was this justification for discarding "the outsider" syndrome? From that time I did and have. I am no longer an "outsider." These are my people because we have the same Father and are organic members of the same Body. I have learned and am still learning much from them. Spontaneous agape love enfolds and embraces us and we are one. I expect to be with them until the rapture. The problem of fellowship between Charismatics and this non-tongues-speaking Charismatic has been solved. My "spiritual odyssey" has ended. *Agape love has bridged the gap.*

ADDENDUM

Faber's "On Judging Others"

The author considers the following a most valuable supplement to Chapter 9. It is taken from *A Pot of Oil* by Dr. George C. Watson, republished by J. Edwin Newby and used by permission.[7]

With regard to our judgment of others, we may safely say there has never lived a Christian that did not, at some time, have to repent for judging his fellows too harshly. And, on the other hand, there never has lived a Christian that ever had to repent of being too loving, compassionate, or charitable. Frederick W. Faber in one of his books, writing on the different classes of believers, has some excellent remarks on the judging of others which I think are very helpful, and so omitting those phrases which are peculiar to Catholics, and compiling his thoughts from different pages, I will give the reader the substance of his remarks.

1. It is a universal law that when we judge others, whether individuals or multitudes, we come to erroneous conclusions from the mere fact that we naturally judge over-harshly. It is one of the effects of our fallen nature to put the worst construction upon what we see or hear about others, and to make small, if any, allowance for the hidden good that is in them. Also, we unwittingly judge of others by the worst parts of our own disposition, and not by the best. It is natural for us to judge of ourselves by the best things in us, but we judge of others by

the worst things in us. It is so common to impute our evil to others, but to think our goodness is peculiarly our own.

2. Severity is one of the natural accompaniments of a young and immature state of grace. Many religious people think that the power to detect evil in others is a special gift from God, to be prized and cultivated, and if such people are inclined to hunt for evil they can always find it to their satisfaction; but the practice begets a habit of suspicion which is utterly ruinous to the deep love of God and to Christlikeness of disposition. Men are never industrious in handing out the good about others, but have a terrific swiftness in seeing the evil; and even religious people, in many instances, have an awful propensity for circulating the evil, but they are very slow to tell the good. It is also a trait among human beings to be most severe with those of their own class, or guild, or profession. Whoever knew a musician to speak commendatory words of another musician? Merchants are severe on merchants. And it is proverbial the world over that religious people are severe on their fellow religionists. This is partly accounted for because each class of mankind is more familiar with the defects, and infirmities, and sins which are liable to affect their class.

3. When we see evil in others, we never can see the amount of inward resistance which the person has given to the evil, or the amount of humiliation and sorrow which they may have for their own failures and defects. The violence of temptation is always invisible, and its peculiar oppressiveness,

owing to heredity, or education, or previous modes of life, can never be estimated by a fellow creature. There are depths of invincible ignorance, not only in the intellectual nature but in man's moral nature, which every individual character has in some one or more directions, and it is almost universally true that even among good religious people there is one point of moral excellence upon which they seem stupid. This explains why we meet so many very excellent people who seem to have some one glaring inconsistency—and everybody has some inconsistency, only they all have not the deep humility to see it. In judging others we fail to see how many odd crossings there are in people's minds, which tell upon their motives and hamper the free action of their moral sense. Much sin lies at the door of a warped mind, but how much guilt there is in the sin can be known to God alone. The heart is the jewel that He covets for His crown, and if the habitual attitude of the heart is better than any particular action which we see, God be praised for it. The fall of man is so great that in this present world it may be there is no one entirely free from obliquity in the perception of perfect, universal justice.

4. The evil in our fellows strikes us with bold, startling proportions, whereas goodness is more quiet and hidden, and often passes unobserved as a very tame affair. It must be observed that evil, of its own nature, is more visible than goodness. Evil is like the world—on the self-defensive; goodness partakes of the nature of God and imitates the ways of God, of quietness, unobtrusiveness, slowness, non-

combativeness, meekly suffers instead of defending itself, and is saturated with the Spirit of God in his feelings and conduct.

The evil we see, or think we see, in others is easily recognized, but oftentimes the people we are judging are more keenly alive to their defects than we imagine, and may grieve over them in secret and feel in their hearts a humiliation and sorrow for them which we cannot know of, for if sorrow for evil were ostentatious and glaring, that would destroy its true character. God has so contrived the moral world that the greater part of goodness must of necessity be hidden like Himself. There are many things that baffle our judgment as to the sincerity of a man's conversion, but we may depend upon it that in a thousand spots which look to us like desert waste, God's mercy is finding something there for His glory.

5. One of the frightful features of the world, and which is hard to dwell upon without some gloom passing over our spirits, is that of the appalling activity of Satan, and under his leadership myriads of demons are incessantly plying our fellow creatures with every possible subtlety and device for their ruin. To judge of others, without taking into consideration the widespread tyranny of evil spirits, would be both unscriptural and unjust. Satan is persecuting the good, even stirring good Christians against good Christians, weaving webs of diplomacy and compromise around the advocates of Christian perfection, or bending all his energies on the ruin of someone who is doing a notable work for

God, or sapping the foundations of a revival church, or causing Christian warriors to misinterpret their orders on the battlefield, in a thousand ways, both with individuals and bodies of men. This terrible work of evil spirits, described by St. Paul in Ephesians, unconsciously affects our judgment of others. But we fail to see that God is ten thousand times more active than Satan, though He seems to be less so. The reason is because we do not know how to follow God in the deep seclusion of His work, for He works opposite to the methods of Satan, and is constantly accomplishing marvelous things in human souls which we do not suspect, because we are not heavenly-minded enough to trace the footprints of His operations. If we actually saw what God is doing in the very people we often criticize and condemn, we could be utterly astonished at the immensity, the vigor, and the versatility of the magnificent spiritual work which God is doing all around us in the world.

Satan is active, but grace is more active. If the vigor of God abides in every atom of the inanimate world, shall we doubt that His presence pervades and controls in the world of human souls, by the energies of an all-wise Providence, beyond all our conjecture, especially when all His majestic operations have for their simple end the accomplishment of infinite love?

6. We see the evil in our fellows much sooner than the good. On a very short acquaintance with persons we discover their defects, and the things in them which are disagreeable to us, and soon find the

weak point in them where they are most likely to fall; but their better nature is more slowly unfolding itself. This invisible character of goodness is not so obtrusive as defects, because there is an instinctive bashfulness in real goodness, even without a man's intending it. When we know people a long while, especially if we love them, there is apt to be the continual breaking forth of virtues in them we never dreamed they possessed; and oftentimes in little things, in the ordinary wear and tear of life, there will come forth in unostentatious ways traits of humility and self-depreciation, or a patience, and sweetness, and unselfishness beyond what we expect of them.

7. In our opinions of others we fail to distinguish between the sinfulness of sin and the deformity which has resulted from sin. There are many things in truly good people that are extremely disagreeable, which may not involve real sin, and it is this disagreeableness or deformity which spreads itself out and covers a greater extent in our estimation of people than does their actual sin, for this deformity infects the manners, taints the tone and atmosphere of a person, and altogether makes a much greater show than real sin. We judge people, not so much by how they stand to God as by the inconvenient or disagreeable way in which they may stand to us.

Much that the eye catches, which is offensive to our moral sense, may not be real sin, and yet we condemn it with a bitterness and severity much more than the real sin which does not happen to interfere with our interests or personal tastes.

This is why an impartial God must condemn us so often for the very condemnation we give to others, because our judgments do not proceed from the love of God but from personal taste. Goodness always tends to be graceful, but in this life there are always to each man a thousand causes which prevent or delay a work of grace in the heart from becoming graceful in life. Grace may work instantaneously, but gracefulness in the details of life operates more slowly, at least in the majority of cases.

8. Nothing is more amazing than the patient, gentle charity that God displays to His creatures. There is something adorable in the compassion of God for mankind which looks like a voluntary blindness to their evil. He seems either not to see, or not to appreciate, the utter unworthiness of man; at least, He goes on His way as though He did not see it. The Bible is full of instances of this in His dealings with both nations and individuals, where His justice seems to move with tortoise pace, constantly pursuing but seemingly on purpose to be a long while catching up with the one to be punished, as if to give him every allowance possible to infinite mercy. Now, the more we are with God, and the closer our union is with Him, and the more deeply we drink of the interior sweetness of His life, the more we shall catch something of His gentleness and compassion of spirit which will destroy our proclivity for harsh judgments and take away the keenness by which we discover evil in others. Even where judgments are legitimate and unavoidable, we may lay it down as a rule that the severity of our

judgments is an infallible index to the lowness of our spiritual state. Green sanctity is ever swift and sharp and thinks God is too lenient, and often acts as if His judgment throne wanted an occupant.

Mature, mellow sanctity is always slow, gentle, and compassionate, making allowances for others which it never feels justified in making for itself. We must therefore be on our guard: for the more severe we are, the lower we are in love, and in proportion as we get milder to others we are strict with self.

The gospel nowhere tells us that sinners are punished to the utmost of their demerits, but it does tell us that the righteous shall be rewarded "with good measure, and shaken together, and running over"; so it is in the rewards of goodness that our merciful Creator seems bent on doing His uttermost.

"David DuPlesis and I have read your manuscript. We are both delighted."
  Ronald C. Haus—President "John 17:21"

"The message that you are presenting in *LOVE COVERS* is one that the Church needs urgently. You speak to all segments of the Church. Let me commend you for your courage."
  Dr. Philip Crouch,
  Former Pres. Central Bible College
  Springfield, Mo.

"This volume is a CLASSIC in Christian literature."
  Ras Robinson—Editor FULNESS MAGAZINE
  Fort Worth, Texas

"I agree with it from start to finish."
  Dr. J .C. Wenger—Head of the Dept. of Historical Theology, Goshen Bible Seminary

"A most important and valuable contribution to the Church of our day."
  Dr. Sherwood Wirt—Editor Emeritus, DECISION Magazine.

"Thank you for the privilege of reading the manuscript of LOVE COVERS. This, I believe, is probably your greatest message, the most timely truth God has given you in view of the crucial hour."

Dr. T. W. Hunt—Professor of Church Music
Southwestern Baptist Theological Seminary